Aug '62   Rutland Vt.   -2

PORTRAITS IN MINIATURE

by Lytton Strachey

ELIZABETH AND ESSEX

QUEEN VICTORIA

EMINENT VICTORIANS

BOOKS & CHARACTERS

PORTRAITS
IN MINIATURE

AND OTHER ESSAYS
BY
LYTTON STRACHEY

HARCOURT, BRACE AND COMPANY

NEW YORK

Typography by Robert S. Josephy

PRINTED IN THE UNITED STATES OF AMERICA
BY QUINN & BODEN COMPANY, INC., RAHWAY, N. J.

*Est brevitate opus, ut currat sententia, neu se
Impediat verbis lassas onerantibus aures.*

HOR. I. SAT. X.

These essays are reprinted by kind permission of the Editors of The New Republic, The Saturday Review, and The Herald Tribune "Books."

Contents

CONTENTS

PORTRAITS IN MINIATURE

Sir John Harington

AN OLD miniature shows a young man's face, whimsically Elizabethan, with tossed-back curly hair, a tip-tilted nose, a tiny point of a beard, and a long single earring, falling in sparkling drops over a ruff of magnificent proportions. Such was John Harington, as he appeared in the happy fifteen-eighties, at Greenwich, or at Nonesuch—a courtier, a wit, a scholar, a poet, and a great favourite with the ladies. Even Gloriana herself usually unbent when he approached her. She liked the foolish fellow. She had known him since he was a child; he was her godson—almost, indeed, a family connection, for his father's first wife had been a natural daughter of her own indefatigable sire. Through this lady the young man had inherited his fine Italian house at Kelston, in Somersetshire, where one day Elizabeth, on her way to Bath, paid him the honour of an extremely expensive visit. He had felt himself obliged to rebuild half the house to lodge his great guest

3

fittingly; but he cared little for that—he wrote a rhyming epigram about it all, which amused the ladies of the bedchamber. He wrote, he found, with extraordinary ease and pleasure; the words came positively running off the end of his pen; and so—to amuse the ladies again, or to tease them—he translated the twenty-eighth book of Ariosto's *Orlando Furioso*, in which the far from decorous history of the fair Fiametta is told. The Queen soon got wind of this. She read the manuscript and sent for the poet. She was shocked, she said, by this attempt to demoralize her household; and she banished the offender from Court until —could there be a more proper punishment?— he should have completed the translation of the whole poem. Harington hurried off to Kelston, worked away for a month or two, and returned with a fine folio containing the entire *Orlando* in English, together with notes, a life of Ariosto, "a general allegory of the whole," and "apologie of Poetrie," an "epistle dedicatorie to the Queenes Majestie," and an engraved title-page with the portrait of himself and his dog Bungay. The book was printed in 1591. The exquisite elegance and mature serenity of the original are nowhere to be found in

4

it; but Harington himself, bringing with him the natural abundance, the charming ingenuousness, the early morning freshness of his wonderful generation, comes to us delightfully on every page.

The translation was well received, and the gay young man looked about for new worlds to conquer. Not to be talked of was his only fear. A curious notion struck him. His nose was sensitive as well as impudent, and he had been made to suffer agonies by the sanitary arrangements in the houses of the great. Suddenly inspired, he invented the water-closet. Then, seizing his pen, he concocted a pamphlet after the manner of Rabelais—or, as he preferred to call him, "the reverent Rabbles"—in which extravagant spirits, intolerable puns, improper stories, and sly satirical digs at eminent personages were blended together into a preposterous rhapsody, followed by an appendix—written, of course, by his servant—could a gentleman be expected to discuss such details?—containing a minute account, with measurements, diagrams and prices, of the new invention. *The Metamorphosis of Ajax*—for so the book, with a crowningly deplorable pun, was entitled—created some sensation. Queen Elizabeth was amused.

But then some malicious courtier told her that one of the satirical digs was aimed at the memory of Leicester, whereupon her smiles changed to frowns, the Star Chamber was talked of, and Harington made a strategic retreat to Somersetshire. "The merry poet, my godson," the Queen declared, "must not come to Greenwich, till he hath grown sober and leaveth the ladies' sports and frolics." But before very long she relented. With her supreme sense of the practical, she saw that, as she put it, "the marrow of the book" was not entirely ludicrous; she sent down word to the poet that she approved of his invention; and eventually she set the fashion for the new contrivances by installing one of them in Richmond Palace, with a copy of the *Ajax* hanging from the wall.

Harington's next adventure was more serious. He was summoned by Essex to join his ill-fated expedition to Ireland, in command of a troop of horse. In Ireland, with a stretch of authority which was bitterly resented by the Queen, Harington was knighted by the rash Lord Deputy, and afterwards, when disaster came thick upon disaster, he followed his patron back to London. In fear and trembling, he presented himself before

6

the enraged Elizabeth. "What!" she cried, "did
the fool bring you too?" The terrified poet fell
upon his knees, while the Queen, as he afterwards
described it, "chafed much, walked fastly to and
fro, and looked with discomposure in her visage."
Then, suddenly rushing towards him, she caught
hold of his girdle. "By God's Son," she shouted,
"I am no Queen, and that man is above me!"
His stammering excuses were cut short with a
"Go back to your business!" uttered in such a
tone that Sir John, not staying to be bidden twice,
fled out of the room, and fled down to Kelston,
"as if all the Irish rebels had been at his heels."

It is clear that poor Harington never quite recovered from the shock of that terrific scene. The
remainder of his life passed in ineffectiveness and
disillusionment. In the bosom of his family he did
his best to forget the storms and shipwrecks of "the
Essex coast"; he wrote incessantly; he cracked
scandalous jokes with his mother-in-law, old Lady
Rogers; he busied himself over the construction of
a curious lantern for King James of Scotland. But
his happy vein had deserted him. His *Discourse
shewing that Elyas must personally come before the Day
of Judgment* could never get finished, and he threw

7

aside his *Treatise on Playe* as a failure. His epigrams, no doubt, were more successful; he scribbled them down on every possible occasion, and the most scurrilous he invariably dispatched to old Lady Rogers. She roared with laughter, but omitted to leave him a legacy. He dashed into her house as she was dying, broke open the chests, tried to get possession of everything, and was at last ignominiously ejected by his brother-in-law. King James was equally disappointing. Even the curious lantern, even a learned, elaborate, and fantastic dissertation *On the Succession to the Crown*, failed to win him. After he had been a year in London, the new King granted Sir John an interview, but, though his Majesty was polite, he was not impressed. "Sir John," he said, with much gravity, "do you truly understand why the Devil works more with ancient women than others?" And, unluckily, on that, Sir John "could not refrain from a scurvy jest." Nevertheless, though he felt that he had made no headway, he would not despair; a little later, the Lord Chancellorship of Ireland and the Archbishopric of Dublin fell vacant, and the author of *Ajax* bravely requested that he should be appointed to both offices. Oddly

8

enough, his application received no answer. He
solaced himself with an endeavour to win the
good graces of the young Prince Henry, to whom
he addressed a discourse, full of pleasant anecdotes, concerning all the bishops of his acquaintance, followed by a letter describing "the good
deedes and straunge feats" of his "rare Dogge,"
Bungay—how he used to carry messages from
London to Kelston, and how, on one occasion,
he took a pheasant from a dish at the Spanish
Ambassador's table, and then returned it to the
very same dish, at a secret sign from his master.

But in truth the days of Bungay were over, and
the new times were uncomfortable and strange.
"I ne'er did see such lack of good order, discre-
tion, and sobriety." There had been jollities and
junketings, no doubt, in his youth, but surely,
they were different. He remembered the "hero-
icall dames," the "stately heroyns" whom he had
celebrated aforetime—

These entertayn great Princes; these have learned
    The tongues, toys, tricks of Rome, of Spayn, of
        Fraunce;
    These can correntos and lavoltas daunce,
And though they foote it false 'tis ne'er discerned.

9

More and more his thoughts reverted to his old mistress. "When she smiled, it was a pure sunshine, that every one did choose to bask in, if they could; but anon came a storm from a sudden gathering of clouds, and the thunder fell in wondrous manner on all alike." Yes! Those were great times indeed! And now . . . he was "olde and infirme"; he was forty-five; he must seek a quiet harbour and lay up his barque. He lingered at Kelston, impoverished, racked by various diseases; he vainly took the Bath waters; he became "stricken of a dead palsy"; until, in 1612, at the age of fifty-one, he passed into oblivion. And in oblivion he has remained. Nobody reads his *Orlando;* his letters are known to none but a few learned historians; his little books of epigrams lie concealed in the grim recesses of vast libraries; and Englishmen today, reflecting on many things, as they enjoy the benefits of a sanitary system unknown to the less fortunate inhabitants of other countries, give never a thought to Sir John Harington.

Muggleton

NEVER did the human mind attain such a magnificent height of self-assertiveness as in England about the year 1650. Then it was that the disintegration of religious authority which had begun with Luther reached its culminating point. The Bible, containing the absolute truth as to the nature and the workings of the Universe, lay open to all; it was only necessary to interpret its assertions; and to do so all that was wanted was the decision of the individual conscience. In those days the individual conscience decided with extraordinary facility. Prophets and prophetesses ranged in crowds through the streets of London, proclaiming, with complete certainty, the explanation of everything. The explanations were extremely varied: so much the better—one could pick and choose. One could become a Behmenist, a Bidellian, a Coppinist, a Salmonist, a Dipper, a Traskite, a Tryonist, a Philadelphian, a Christadelphian, or a Seventh Day Baptist, just as one pleased. Samuel Butler might fleer and flout at

> petulant, capricious sects,
> The maggots of corrupted texts;

but he, too, was deciding according to the light of
his individual conscience. By what rule could men
determine whether a text was corrupted, or what
it meant? The rule of the Catholic Church was
gone, and henceforward Eternal Truth might
with perfect reason be expected to speak through
the mouth of any fish-wife in Billingsgate.

Of these prophets the most famous was George
Fox; the most remarkable was Lodowick Muggleton. He was born in 1609, and was brought up to
earn his living as a tailor. Becoming religious, he
threw over a charming girl, with whom he was in
love and whom he was engaged to marry, on the
ground that her mother kept a pawnbroker's shop
and that usury was sinful. He was persuaded to
this by his puritan friends, among whom was his
cousin, John Reeve, a man of ardent temperament, fierce conviction, and unflinching holiness.
Some years later, in 1650, two peculiar persons,
John Tawny and John Robins, appeared in London. Tawny declared that he was the Lord's high

priest, that it was his mission to lead the Jews back to Jerusalem, and that, incidentally, he was the King of France. Robins proclaimed that he was something greater: he was Adam, he was Melchizedek, he was the Lord himself. He had raised Jeremiah, Benjamin, and many others from the dead, and did they not stand there beside him, admitting that all he said was true? Serpents and dragons appeared at his command; he rode upon the wings of the wind; he was about to lead 144,000 men and women to the Mount of Olives through the Red Sea, on a diet of dry bread and raw vegetables. These two men, "greater than prophets," made a profound impression upon Muggleton and his cousin Reeve. A strange melancholy fell upon them, and then a more strange exaltation. They heard mysterious voices; they were holy; why should not they too be inspired? Greater than prophets . . . ? Suddenly Reeve rushed into Muggleton's room and declared that they were the chosen witnesses of the Lord, whose appearance had been prophesied in the Book of Revelation, xi. 3. Muggleton agreed that it was so. As for Tawny and Robins, they were devilish impostors, who must be immediately denounced.

13

Sentence of eternal damnation should be passed
upon them. The cousins hurried off on their mission, and discovered Robins in gaol, where he had
been lodged for blasphemy. The furious embodi-
ment of Adam, Melchizedek, and the Lord glared
out at them from a window, clutching the bars
with both hands. But Reeve was unabashed.
"That body of thine," he shouted, pointing at his
victim, "which was thy heaven, must be thy hell;
and that proud spirit of thine, which said it was
God, must be thy Devil. The one shall be as fire,
and the other as brimstone, burning together to
all eternity. This is the message of the Lord." The
effect was instantaneous: Robins, letting go the
bars, fell back, shattered. "It is finished," he
groaned; "the Lord's will be done." He wrote a
letter to Cromwell, recanting; was released from
prison, and retired into private life, in the depths
of the country. Tawny's fate was equally impressive. Reeve wrote on a piece of paper, "We pass
sentence upon you of eternal damnation," and
left it in his room. The wretched man fled to Holland, in a small boat, *en route* for Jerusalem, and
was never heard of again.

After this the success of the new religion was

assured. But Reeve did not live long to enjoy his glory. In a few months his fiery spirit had worn itself away, and Muggleton was left alone to carry on the work. He was cast in a very different mould. Tall, thick-set, vigorous, with a great head, whose low brow, high cheekbones, and projecting jowl almost suggested some Simian creature, he had never known a day's illness, and lived to be eighty-eight. Tough and solid, he continued, year after year, to earn his living as a tailor, while the words flowed from him which were the final revelation of God. For he preached and he wrote with an inexhaustible volubility. IIe never ceased, in sermons, in letters, in books, in pamphlets, to declare to the world the divine and absolute truth. His revelations might be incomprehensible, his objurgations frenzied, his argumentations incoherent—no matter; disciples gathered round him in ever-thickening crowds, learning, to their amazement and delight, that there is no Devil but the unclean Reason of men, that Angels are the only beings of Pure Reason, that God is of the stature of a man and made of flesh and bone, that Heaven is situated beyond the stars and six miles above the earth. Schismatics might arise, but they were crushed, cast forth, and sentenced to eternal damnation. Inquiring magistrates were browbeaten with multitudinous texts. George Fox, the miserable wretch, was overwhelmed—or would have been had he not obtained the assistance of the Devil—by thick volumes of intermingled abuse and Pure Reason. The truth was plain—it had been delivered to Muggleton by God; and henceforward, until the Day of Judgment, the Deity would hold no further communication with his creatures. Prayer, therefore, was not only futile, it was blasphemous; and no form of worship was admissible, save the singing of a few hymns of thanksgiving and praise. All that was required of the true believer was that he should ponder upon the Old and the New Testaments, and upon "The Third and Last Testament of Our Lord Jesus Christ," by Muggleton.

The English passion for compromise is well illustrated by the attitude of Charles the Second's Government towards religious heterodoxy. There are two logical alternatives for the treatment of heretics—to let them alone, or to torture them to death; but English public opinion recoiled—it still recoils—from either course. A compromise

was the obvious, the comfortable solution; and so
it was decided that heretics should be tortured—
not to death, oh no!—but . . . to some extent.
Accordingly, poor Muggleton became a victim,
for years, to the small persecutions of authority.
He was badgered by angry justices, he was hunted
from place to place, his books were burnt, he was
worried by small fines and short imprisonments.
At last, at the age of sixty-eight, he was arrested
and tried for blasphemy. In the course of the proceedings, it appeared that the prosecution had
made a serious blunder: since the publication of
the book on which the charge was based an Act
of Indemnity had been passed. Thereupon the
Judge instructed the jury that, as there was no
reason to suppose that the date on the book was
not a false imprint, the Act of Indemnity did not
apply; and Muggleton was condemned to the
pillory. He was badly mauled, for it so happened
that the crowd was hostile and pelted the old man
with stones. After that, he was set free; his tribu-
lations were at last over. The Prophet spent his
closing years writing his autobiography, in the
style of the Gospels; and he died in peace.

His doctrines did not die with him. Two hundred and fifty Muggletonians followed him to the grave, and their faith has been handed down, unimpaired through the generations, from that day to this. Still, in the very spot where their founder was born, the chosen few meet together to celebrate the two festivals of their religion—the Great Holiday, on the anniversary of the delivery of the Word to Reeve, and the Little Holiday, on the day of Muggleton's final release from prison.

> I do believe in God alone,
> Likewise in Reeve and Muggleton.

So they have sung for more than two hundred years.

> This is the Muggletonians' faith,
> This is the God which we believe;
> None salvation-knowledge hath
> But those of Muggleton and Reeve.
> Christ is the Muggletonians' king,
> With whom eternally they'll sing.

It is an exclusive faith, certainly; and yet, somehow or other, it disarms criticism. Even though one may not be of the elect oneself, one cannot but wish it well; one would be sorry if the time ever came when there were no more Muggletonians. Besides, one is happy to learn that with the passage of years they have grown more gentle. Their terrible offensive weapon—which, in early days, they wielded so frequently—has fallen into desuetude: no longer do they pass sentence of eternal damnation. The dreaded doom was pronounced for the last time on a Swedenborgian, with great effect, in the middle of the nineteenth century.

John Aubrey

IF ONE were asked to choose a date for the beginning of the modern world, probably July 15,
1662, would be the best to fix upon. For on that
day the Royal Society was founded, and the place
of Science in civilization became a definite and
recognized thing. The sun had risen above the
horizon; and yet, before that, there had been
streaks of light in the sky. The great age of Newton was preceded by a curious twilight period—a
period of gestation and preparation, confused,
and only dimly conscious of the end towards
which it was moving. It might be called, perhaps,
the age of Hobbes, whose half-mediaeval, half-
modern mind was the dominating influence over
intellects which came to maturity in the middle
years of the century. Another even more typical,
though less eminent, representative of this em-
bryonic generation was John Aubrey (1626–1697).
Aubrey was among those chosen by the first Presi-
dent and Council to be the first Fellows of the

Royal Society; and he was extremely proud of the distinction. But in reality the scientific movement which gave the Royal Society its significance did not mean very much to him. His mind moved in a circle of ideas which was rapidly becoming obsolete, and which, so long as our civilization lasts, can never come into existence again.

His life was not a fortunate one. Born a country gentleman, with estates in Brecknockshire, Herefordshire, and Wiltshire, and educated at Trinity College, Oxford, his happy studies at the University were interrupted by the Civil Wars, and his considerable possessions were dissipated in a long series of unsuccessful lawsuits. In 1666, he tells us, "all my businesses and affaires ran kim kam; nothing tooke effect"; and the words are applicable to the whole of his life. It was not only luck that was against him; he was by nature an amiable muddler; in love and in literature, no less than in business, it was always the same—"nothing tooke effect." Neither Madam Jane Codrington, nor "that incomparable good conditioned gentlewoman, Mris. M. Wiseman, with whom at first sight I was in love," would smile upon him; and though "domina Katherina Ryves," with a dowry of £2,000, was kinder, just as she was about to marry him she died. He sought distraction abroad, but without success. "1664, in August," he noted, "had a terrible fit of the spleen, and piles, at Orleans." Yet worse was to follow: "In an ill howre," he began to make his addresses to Joan Sumner, whose cruelty was more than negative. She had him arrested in Chancery Lane, and for three years pursued him with lawsuits. His ruin followed; all his broad lands vanished; even Easton Piers, the house of his birth, with its terraced gardens, its "jedeau," its grotto and "volant Mercury," had to be sold; even his books went at last. By 1670 poor Aubrey had lost everything. But then, unexpectedly, happiness descended upon him. Free at last from the struggles of love and law and the tedious responsibilities of property, he found himself in a "sweet *otium*." "I had never quiett, nor anything of happiness till divested of all," he wrote. "I was in as much affliction as a mortall could bee, and never quiet till all was gone, and I wholly cast myselfe on God's providence."

God's providence, in Aubrey's case, took the form of a circle of kindly friends, who were ready enough to give him food and shelter in town and country, in return for the benefit of his "most ingeniose conversation." He would spend the winter in London—often with Sir William Petty or Sir Christopher Wren,—and then, with the spring, he would ride off on a round of visits—to Lord Thanet's in Kent, to the Longs in Wiltshire, to Edmund Wylde in Shropshire—until the autumn came, and he would turn his horse's head back to London. Grumpy Anthony Wood might write him down "a shiftless person, roving and magotie-headed, and sometimes little better than crazed"; but his boon companions thought otherwise. They relished to the full the extraordinary quantity and the delightful variety of his information, and could never tire of his engaging manner of presenting it. "My head," he said himself, "was always working; never idle, and even travelling did glean som observations, of which I have a collection in folio of 2 quiers of paper and a dust basket, some whereof are to be valued." His inquiries were indeed indefatigable; he was learned in natural history, geology, Gothic architecture, mineralogy, painting, heraldry; he collected statistics, he was a profound astrologer, and a learned geometrician; he wrote a treatise on education; even the mysteries of cookery did not elude him, and he compiled "a collection of approved receipts." Before he died he had written sufficient to fill several volumes; but, characteristically enough, he brought only one book to the point of publication: his *Miscellanies*, in which he briefly discussed such fascinating subjects as "Apparitions, Impulses, Knockings, Blows Invisible, Prophecies, Marvels, Magic, Transportation in the Air, Visions in a Bevil or Glass, Converse with Angels and Spirits, Corps-Candles in Wales, Glances of Love and Envy, and Second-Sighted Persons in Scotland." It is in this book, in the chapter on Apparitions, that the sentence occurs which so much delighted Mr. Jonathan Oldbuck of Monkbarns: "*Anno* 1670, not far from *Cirencester*, was an Apparition; Being demanded, whether a good Spirit, or a bad? Returned no answer, but disappeared with a curious Perfume and most melodious Twang."

Certainly the learned Ray was right when he said of his friend that he was "a little inclinable to credit strange relations." Yet it would be an error to dismiss Aubrey as a mere superstitious trifler; he was something more interesting than

24

that. His insatiable passion for singular odds and ends had a meaning in it; he was groping towards a scientific ordering of phenomena; but the twilight of his age was too confusing, and he could rarely distinguish between a fact and a fantasy. He was clever enough to understand the Newtonian system, but he was not clever enough to understand that a horoscope was an absurdity; and so, in his crowded curiosity-shop of a brain, astronomy and astrology both found a place, and were given equal values. When fortune favoured him, however, he could make real additions to knowledge. He was the first English archaeologist, and his most remarkable achievement was the discovery of the hitherto unknown Druidical temple of Avebury. Encouraged by Charles II, he made a careful survey of the great stone circle, writing a dissertation upon it and upon Stonehenge, and refuting the theory of Inigo Jones, who, in order to prove that the latter was Roman, had given an entirely factitious account of it. As he rode over the Wiltshire downs, hawking with Colonel Long, he had ample opportunities for these antiquarian investigations. "Our sport," he wrote, "was very good, and in a romantick coun-

25

trey, for the prospects are noble and vast, the downs stockt with numerous flocks of sheep, the turfe rich and fragrant with thyme and burnet; nor are the nut-brown shepherdesses without their graces. But the flight of the falcons was but a parenthesis to the Colonell's facetious discourse, who was *tam Marti quam Mercurio*, and the Muses did accompany him with his hawkes and spaniells."

The country was charming; but London too was full of pleasures, and the winter nights passed swiftly with wine and talk. For the company was excellent. There was Robert Hooke "that invented the Pendulum-Watches, so much more useful than the other watches," and a calculating machine, and hundreds of other contrivances—"he believes not fewer than a thousand"—and who declared he had forestalled Mr. Newton; and there was Dr. Tonge, who had first taught children to write by means of copper-plates, and left behind him "two tomes in folio of alchymy"; and Francis Potter, the first to practise the transfusion of blood, who, at 10 o'clock in the morning of December 10, 1625, as he was going upstairs, had discovered "the mysterie of the Beaste"; and John Pell, the inventor of the division-sign in arith-

metic, who "haz sayd to me that he did believe
that he solved some questions *non sine divino aux-
ilio.*" And then the gentle gossip went back to
earlier days—to old Mr. Oughtred, Sir Christopher's master, who "taught all free," and was an
astrologer, though he confessed "that he was not
satisfied how it came about that one might fore-
tell by the starres, but so it was," and whose "wife
was a penurious woman, and would not allow
him to burne candle after supper, by which
meanes many a good notion is lost, and many a
problem unsolved"; and so back to a still more
remote and bizarre past—to Dr. John Dee, of
Queen Elizabeth's time, "who wore a gowne like
an artist's gowne, with hanging sleeves and a slit,"
made plates of gold "by projection," and "used
to distil eggeshells."

Aubrey lived on into old age—vague, precise,
idle, and busy to the last. His state of life, he felt,
was not quite satisfactory. He was happy; but he
would have been happier still in some other world.
He regretted the monasteries. He wished "the re-
formers had been more moderate on that point."
It was "fitt there should be receptacles and pro-
vision for contemplative men"; and "what a pleas-

ure 'twould have been to have travelled from monastery to monastery!" As it was, he did the next best thing—he travelled from country house to country house. In the summer of 1697, when he was over seventy, as he was riding through Oxford on his way to Lady Long's, he was seized with sudden illness, and his journeying was ended for ever.

In the great mass of papers that he left behind him it was hardly to be supposed that there could be anything of permanent value. Most of the antique science was already out of date at his death. But it so happened that Aubrey's appetite for knowledge had carried him into a field of inquiry which, little explored in his own day, attracts the greatest interest in ours. He was an assiduous biographer. Partly to help the ungrateful Anthony Wood in the compilation of his *Athenae Oxonienses*, but chiefly for his own delight, Aubrey was in the habit of jotting down on scraps of paper every piece of information he could acquire concerning both his own contemporaries and the English worthies of previous generations. He was accurate, he had an unfailing eye for what was interesting, and he possessed—it was almost inevitable in those days—a natural gift of style. The result is that his *Short Lives* (which have been admirably edited for the Clarendon Press by Mr. Andrew Clark) are not only an authority of the highest importance upon seventeenth-century England, but one of the most readable of books. A biography should either be as long as Boswell's or as short as Aubrey's. The method of enormous and elaborate accretion which produced the *Life of Johnson* is excellent, no doubt; but, failing that, let us have no half-measures; let us have the pure essentials—a vivid image, on a page or two, without explanations, transitions, commentaries, or padding. This is what Aubrey gives us; this, and one thing more—a sense of the pleasing, anxious being who, with his odd old alchemy, has transmuted a few handfuls of orts and relics into golden life.

The Life, Illness, and Death
of Dr. North

JOHN NORTH was a man of eminence in his day
—a prebend of Westminster, Professor of Greek
at Cambridge, Master of Trinity College, and
Clerk of the King's Closet: now totally forgotten.
Only the curious inquirer, chancing on the obscure and absurd memoir of him by his admiring
younger brother, Roger, catches a glimpse of the
intense individual existence of this no longer distinguished man. In the sight of God, we used to
be told, a thousand years are as a day; possibly;
but notions of the deity are not what they were in
the days of King David and Sir Isaac Newton;
Evolution, the Life Force, and Einstein have all
intervened; so that whether the dictum is still one
to which credence should be attached is a problem that must be left to Professor Whitehead (who
has studied the subject very carefully) to determine. However that may be, for mortal beings
the case is different. In their sight (or perhaps one

should say their blindness) a thousand years are too liable to be not as a day but as just nothing. The past is almost entirely a blank. The indescribable complexities, the incalculable extravagances, of a myriad consciousnesses have vanished for ever. Only by sheer accident, when some particular drop from the ocean of empty water is slipped under the microscope—only when some Roger North happens to write a foolish memoir, which happens to survive, and which we happen to open—do we perceive for an amazed moment or two the universe of serried and violent sensations that lies concealed so perfectly in the transparency of oblivion.

Born in 1645, the younger son of an impecunious peer, John North was one of those good little boys who, in the seventeenth century, were invariably destined to Learning, the Universities, and the Church. His goodness, his diligence, his scrupulosity, were perhaps, it is true, the result of a certain ingrained timidity rather than anything else; but that could not be helped. Fear is not easily exorcised. As an undergraduate at Cambridge the youth was still afraid of ghosts in the dark, and slept with the bedclothes over his head. "For some time," we are told, "he lay with his Tutor, who once, coming home, found the Scholar in bed with only his Crown visible. The Tutor, indiscreetly enough, pulled him by the Hair; whereupon the Scholar sunk down, and the Tutor followed, and at last, with a great Outcry, the Scholar sprung up, expecting to see an enorm Spectre." But in spite of such contretemps the young man pursued his studies with exemplary industry. He was soon a Fellow of his college and a Doctor of Divinity. He continued to work and work; collected a vast library; read the Classics until "Greek became almost vernacular to him"; wrestled with Hebrew, dived deep into Logic and Metaphysics, and was even "a Friend to, though no great Scholar in, the Mathematicks." Unwilling to waste a moment of time, the Doctor found means for turning the most ordinary conversations into matter for improvement, but "he could not be pleased with such insipid Pastime as Bowls, or less material Discourse, such as Town Tales, Punning, and the Like." At last his fame as a prodigy of learning spread over the land. He preached before King Charles II, and the great Duke of Lauderdale became his patron. At the early age of twenty-seven, his talents and virtues were rewarded by the Professorship of Greek in the University of Cambridge.

His talents and virtues were indeed great; but still they were informed and dominated by an underlying apprehensiveness. Meticulous, in the true sense of the word, was the nature of the Doctor. An alarmed exactitude kept him continually on the stretch. He was in fear alike for the state of his soul and for his reputation with posterity. He published only one small volume—a commentary on some of Plato's Dialogues; all the rest of the multitudinous fruits of his labours—notes, sermons, treatises, lectures, dissertations—were burnt, by his direction, after his death. A small note-book alone survived by accident, containing the outline of a great work against Socinians, Republics, and Hobbes. But the Doctor had taken care to write on the first page of it—"I beshrew his heart, that gathers my opinion from anything he finds wrote here." Nor was this strange diffidence merely literary; it extended to his person as well. He would never allow his portrait to be painted, in spite of the entreaties of Sir Peter Lely; "and, what was very odd, he would not leave the

33

Print in his Bed, where he had lain, remain un-
defaced."

Curiously enough, his appearance seemed to
belie his character. His complexion was florid, his
hair flaxen, and, "as some used to jest, his
Features were scandalous, as showing rather a
Madam *entravestie* than a Book-Worm." At times,
indeed, it almost appeared as if his features were
a truer index to his soul than the course of his life.
His friends were surprised to see that, among his
pupils, he "affected to refresh himself with the
society of the young Noblemen," who gathered
round him, in fits of laughter, "like Younglings
about old *Silenus*." He was arch, too, with the
ladies, plying them with raillery. "Of all the
Beasts of the Field," he said, "God Almighty
thought Woman the fittest Companion for Man";
and the ladies were delighted. But unfortunately
no corresponding specimen of his jests with the
young noblemen has been preserved.

In 1677, when he was thirty-two, his career
reached its climax, and he was made Master of
Trinity. The magnificent appointment proved to
be his ruin. Faced with the governance of the
great college over which the omniscient Barrow

had lately ruled and which the presence of Newton still made illustrious, the Doctor's sense of responsibility, of duty, and of inadequacy became almost pathological. His days and his nights passed in one ceaseless round of devotion, instruction, and administration, reading, writing, and abstemiousness. He had no longer any time for the young and the fair; no time for a single particle of enjoyment; no time even for breakfast. His rule was strict beyond all measure and precedent. With relentless severity he pursued the undergraduates through their exercises and punished them for their peccadilloes. His unpopularity became intense: he was openly jeered at in the Cloisters, and one evening a stone came whizzing through the window of the room in the Lodge where he was sitting, and fell in the fire at his feet. Nor was he consoled by the friendship of his equals. The Senior Fellows were infuriated by his sour punctilio; a violent feud sprang up; there were shocking scenes at the council meetings. "Let me be buried in the ante-chapel," exclaimed the Master in his desperation, "so that they may trample on me dead as they have living."

And death was always before his eyes; for now

35

a settled hypochondria was added to his other
miseries. He was a prey to constant nightmare.
He had little doubt that he would perish of the
stone. Taking upon himself the functions of the
Wise Woman, he displayed before his embarrassed friends the obvious symptoms of fatal disorder. "Gravel! Red gravel!" he gasped. In reality
his actual weakness lay in quite another direction.
One day he caught cold, it grew worse, his throat
was affected, his uvula swelled. The inflammation
continued, and before long the unhappy Doctor
became convinced that his uvula would have to
be cut off. All the physicians of the University
were summoned, and they confessed that the case
was grave. It was the age of Molière, and the
practitioners of Cambridge might well have fig-
ured in the "Malade Imaginaire." Their pre-
scriptions were terrific and bizarre: drenches,
"enough to purge a strong man from off his legs,"
accompanied by amber, to be smoked like tobacco
in pipes, with astringent powders blown into the
mouth through quills. The Doctor, who, with all
his voluminous reading, had never heard of Dia-
foirus, believed every word he was told, and carried out the fearful orders with elaborate consci-

entiousness. The result was plain to all; in a few weeks his health was completely shattered, and his friends, to their amazement, saw him "come helmeted in Caps upon Caps, and meagre as one newly crope out of a Fever." They privately consulted the great Dr. Lower in London. He threw up his hands. "I would undertake," he said, "by the smoak of Amber alone, to put the soundest Man in the World into Convulsion Fits." But it was too late to intervene; the treatment was continued, while the Doctor struggled on with the duties of his office. Two scholars were to be publicly admonished for scandalous conduct; the fellows assembled; the youths stood trembling; the Master appeared. Emaciated, ghastly, in his black gown, and with a mountain of caps upon his head, the extraordinary creature began a tirade of bitter and virulent reproof; when suddenly his left leg swerved beneath him, and he fell in a fit upon the ground. It was apoplexy. He was carried to his bed, where the physicians clustered round him. The one thing, they declared, that was essential was that he should never lose consciousness; if he did he would never regain it; and they therefore ordered that a perpetual noise should

37

be made about his ears. Whereupon "there was a Consort of Tongs, Firegrate, Wainscote-Drum, and dancing of Curtains and Curtain Rings, such as would have made a sound Man mad." At that moment, old Lady North, the patient's mother and a formidable dowager, appeared upon the scene. She silenced the incredible tintinnabulation; she even silenced the faculty; and she succeeded in nursing her son back from death.

Yet there were some who averred that it would have been better had she never done so. For now the strangest of the Doctor's transformations came upon him. His recovery was not complete; his body was paralyzed on the left side; but it was in his mind that the most remarkable change had occurred. His fears had left him. His scrupulosity, his diffidence, his seriousness, even his morality —all had vanished. He lay on his bed in reckless levity, pouring forth a stream of flippant observations, and naughty stories, and improper jokes. While his friends hardly knew which way to look, he laughed consumedly, his paralyzed features drawn up into a curiously distorted grin. He sent for a gay young scholar of the college, Mr. Warren, to sit by him and regale him with merry tales and readings from light romances. And there was worse still to follow. Attacked by epileptic seizures, he declared that the only mitigation of his sufferings lay in the continued consumption of wine. He, who had been so noted for his austerities, now tossed off, with wild exhilaration, glass after glass of the strongest sherry; the dry ascetic had become a convert to the golden gospel of *la dive bouteille*. In the depth of the night, the studious precincts of the Great Court of Trinity were disturbed by peculiar sounds—the high, triumphant, one-sided cackle of the Master, as he lay, with his flagon in his hand and young Mr. Warren beside him, absorbed in the abandoned, exuberant fantasies of the Curé of Meudon.

After four years of this strange existence, the Doctor died in his sleep. He was buried, as he had directed, in the ante-chapel of the college, where, under a small square stone, engraved with the initials "J. N.," so many singular agitations came to their final rest. In his brother Roger's opinion, "the Consciousness of a well-spent Life was of great service to him," for otherwise he "might have fallen into Melancholy, Dejections, Despair, and Misconstructions of Providence." And prob-

39

ably Roger was right; conscientiousness is apt, in however devious a manner, to have its reward in this world. Whether it also has it in any other is another of those questions that must be referred to Professor Whitehead.

Congreve, Collier, Macaulay, and Mr. Summers

As the Victorian Age grows dim on the horizon, various neglected luminaries re-emerge—among others the comic dramatists of the Restoration. The work of Sheridan begins to be taken at its true value—as a clever but emasculated *rifacimento;* the supreme master of prose comedy in English is seen to be Congreve. At least, let us hope so. To those who are still in doubt, or in ignorance, the new complete edition of Congreve's works, published by the Nonesuch Press, and edited by Mr. Montague Summers, should bring conviction or conversion. Congreve now appears for the first time as he should have appeared long ago—as classic. The get-up of these four quarto volumes—though it cannot be said to equal the perfect amenity of the Baskerville edition of 1761 —is admirable; and the critical prefaces, notes, and commentaries are a monument of erudition and exactitude. Mr. Summers prints the plays, probably rightly, from the original editions, and not from the last edition published during the author's lifetime, which has formed the basis of all subsequent texts. He thus restores to life several excellent jokes, deleted by Congreve owing to the attacks of Jeremy Collier, though he does so at the cost of relegating various small improvements and polishings to the list of variants; but no doubt—if one must choose—polishings are less valuable than jokes. Another decided gain is the reversion to the original arrangement of the scenes, which had been unnecessarily Frenchified by Congreve himself, and had subsequently undergone a process of serious degradation—still unfortunately visible in the current "Mermaid" edition. Mr. Summers's interesting introduction is full of learning, argument, and feeling—in fact, perhaps too full. There is an idiosyncratic exuberance about it, which sorts ill with the exquisite impersonality of Congreve. To speak of "the disastrous Revolution of 1688," for instance, and to describe the Lollards as "Wyclif's gang," is odd; and oddity should not appear in Congreve's editor. One small point may be mentioned, as an illustration of the dangers which attend an excess of zeal: " 'Tis true we found you and Mr. Fainall in the blue garret," says Mincing, the lady's maid, to Mrs. Marwood; "by the same token, you swore us to secrecy upon Messalina's Poems." Mr. Summers has the following note: " ' Messalina's Poems.' Considerable research has failed to trace this book. It is alluded to before as 'a Book of Verses and Poems,' and I would suggest that it was a collection of obscene lyrics and songs clandestinely printed." Alas, for Mr. Summers's "considerable research"! A word with Millamant would have brought light in a moment. For the explanation is as simple as it is delightful: Mincing had got the title of the "Book of Verses and Poems" just a little wrong; instead of "Messalina's," she should have said "Miscellaneous."

The difficulty of distinguishing between what is Miscellaneous and what is Messalina's is not confined to Mincing. The dividing line has never been absolutely drawn, and learned magistrates are worried with the question to this hour. But at the end of the seventeenth century discussions upon ethics and aesthetics were even more confused and confusing than they are at the present day. For one thing, there were more red herrings

on the track. The divine and mysterious require-
ments of dogmatic theology had to be attended
to—so had the almost equally divine and mysterious pronouncements of Aristotle. Jeremy Collier,
however, was troubled with no doubts. He saw
Messalina everywhere; and, in his *Short View of the
Profaneness and Immorality of the English Stage*, published in 1698, he singled out the dramatists of the
time for a violent castigation. To a modern reader,
Collier's book is nothing but a curiosity, its only
merit being, oddly enough, an aesthetic one—it is
written in good plain English. The arguments
throughout are grotesque, and it is clear that
Collier had never stopped for two minutes to con-
sider the general questions at issue. He supports
his contentions by appeals to Tertullian, Minutius
Felix, St. Chrysostom, and "the Bishop of Arras";
the ancient drama, he gravely maintains, was less
scurrilous than the modern—did not Sophocles
show the deepest respect for oracles? As for his
conception of what constitutes stage immorality,
it is most extraordinary. Any opinion held by any
character in a play is assumed to be the author's.
Congreve is seriously pronounced to be obscene
and blasphemous because he makes his gentlemen

44

say "Pox on't," and his ladies "Jesu!" while Dryden is savagely hectored for "abusing the clergy" because in one of his plays an Egyptian princess rails at the priests of Apis. Obviously, this absurd volume lay open to more than one crushing rejoinder. Several rejoinders were made; but their ineptitude is symptomatic of the age; and the most inept of all was Congreve's. With a strange perversity the wittiest man alive made a complete fool of himself by rushing into the one position that was untenable. He maintained that his plays were not indecent, but that, on the contrary, they were written to subserve the highest ends of virtue. He, too, actually appealed to the Early Fathers. It is impossible to decide which of the two antagonists is the more ridiculous—Collier when he fiercely anathematizes Congreve for calling a coachman Jehu, or Congreve when he blandly assumes that there is nothing improper in Lady Plyant and Mr. Scandal.

Unluckily, the true nature of this preposterous controversy has become obscured by Macaulay. In an essay, written in that style which, with its metallic exactness and its fatal efficiency, was certainly one of the most remarkable products of the

Industrial Revolution, Macaulay has impressed upon the mind of the ordinary reader his own version of the affair. Wishing to make a dramatic story of it, with a satisfactory moral, he has presented Collier as a hero—not, to be sure, without his little shortcomings, but still a hero—who, in the twinkling of an eye, purged not only the English theatre, but English literature itself, of the deplorable and reprehensible grossness which had been disgracing the country for the last forty years. A few inconvenient facts are forgotten—the fact, for instance, that the Restoration Comedies continued to be acted unceasingly throughout the eighteenth century. But, no doubt, it is to the moral revolution effected by the *Short View* that we owe the exquisite propriety of the farces of Fielding and the chaste refinements of *Gulliver's Travels* and the *Dunciad*.

One of the wildest of Macaulay's aberrations is his picture of Collier as a great humorist. As Mr. Summers observes, an utter—a devastating—a positively unnerving lack of humour is the most conspicuous feature of the *Short View*. Yet Macaulay has the effrontery to mention Pascal in connection with this egregious jackass. He was gambling heavily on none of his readers having the curiosity to open the book.

Whether Mr. Summers's account of the dispute will supersede Macaulay's seems to be a little doubtful. He is, perhaps, too much of a partisan. His unwillingness to admit the weakness of Congreve's arguments diminishes the force of his denunciation of Collier's. In truth, the question is not so simple. No doubt, as Mr. Summers says, art and life are different things; but wherein precisely lies the difference? Later, Mr. Summers justifies the comedies of the Restoration on the ground that they were a truthful representation of life as it was lived in the high society of the time. "A close parallel," he adds, "may be found in the decadence of Venice." Surely he might have pushed the comparison a little further—as far as the present day. One can easily think of a Mr. Tattle in Bloomsbury, and a Lady Froth in Mayfair. Nevertheless, it is plainly paradoxical to find in *The Double Dealer* or *The Way of the World* a faithful presentment of any state of society; it is not in that fashion that real life is lived. What, then, is the explanation of this close resemblance combined with this obvious unlikeness? How is it

47

that we are well acquainted with Mrs. Frail, without for a moment supposing that either she or ourselves are figuring in a Congreve comedy? Perhaps the truth is that pure Comedy, unlike Tragedy and Drama and most forms of fiction, depends for its existence on the construction of a conventional world in which, while human nature and human actions are revealed, their consequences are suspended. The characters in Comedy are real; but they exist *in vacuo*. They are there neither to instruct us nor to exalt us, but simply to amuse us; and therefore the effects which would in reality follow from their conduct must not appear. If they did, the comedy would cease to exist: the jealous husband would become a tragic personage; the heavy father a Galsworthy character; the rake would be revealed as a pest, and the old bore as . . . an old bore. By the magic of Comedy, what is scabrous, what is melancholy, what is vicious, and what is tiresome in the actual life of society is converted into charming laughter and glittering delight.

This being so, it is as futile for the comic writer to pretend that he is, in reality, a moralist in disguise, as it is for the moralist to blame the comic

writer for ignoring morality. The true weight of
the moral objection lies in a very different con-
sideration. It is perfectly possible that the presen-
tation of such spectacles as Comedy presents may
prove, in certain circumstances, undermining to
the virtue of the spectators. But it is obvious that
here no general rule can be laid down; everything
depends upon contingencies. The time, the place,
the shifting significations of words, the myriad
dispositions of the audience or the reader—all
these things are variables which can never be reduced to a single formula. Queen Caroline's meat
was Queen Victoria's poison; and perhaps Lord
Macaulay's poison was Mr. Aldous Huxley's pap.
Every case must be considered on its own merits;
but, after all, in any case, such considerations have
no bearing upon the intrinsic excellence of works of
art. Fireworks do not cease to be exhilarating and
beautiful because it is dangerous for inexperienced
governesses to play with them. The comedies of
Congreve must be ranked among the most wonderful and glorious creations of the human mind,
although it is quite conceivable that, in certain circumstances, and at a given moment, a whole bench
of Bishops might be demoralized by their perusal.

Madame de Sévigné's Cousin

MADAME DE SÉVIGNÉ was one of those chosen
beings in whom the forces of life are so
abundant and so glorious that they overflow in
every direction and invest whatever they meet
with the virtue of their own vitality. She was the
sun of a whole system, which lived in her light
—which lives still for us with a kind of reflected
immortality. We can watch—with what a marvellous distinctness!—the planets revolving through
that radiance—the greater and the less, and the
subordinate moons and dimmest asteroids—from
Madame de Grignan herself to the dancing gyp-
sies at Vichy. But then, when the central luminary
is withdrawn, what an incredible convulsion! All
vanish; we are dimly aware for a little of some obscure shapes moving through strange orbits; and
after that there is only darkness.

Emmanuel de Coulanges, for instance. He lived
a long life, filled his own place in the world, married, travelled, had his failures and his successes

. . . but all those happenings were mere phenomena; the only reality about him lay in one
thing—he was Madame de Sévigné's cousin. He
was born when she was seven years old, and he
never knew a time when he had not loved her.
She had petted the little creature when it was a
baby, and she had gone on petting it all her life.
He had not been quite an ordinary child: he had
had strange fancies. There was a fairy, called
Cafut, so he declared, to whom he was devoted;
this was not approved of—it looked like incipient
madness; and several whippings had to be administered before *Cafut* was exorcised. In reality,
no one could have been saner than the little Emmanuel; but he had ways of amusing himself
which seemed unaccountable to the grandly positive generation into which he had been born.
There was something about him which made him
no fit contemporary of Bossuet. Madame de Sévigné, so completely, so magnificently, a child of
her age, while she loved him, could never take
him quite seriously. In her eyes, though he might
grow old, he could not grow up. At the age of
sixty, white-haired and gouty, he remained for
her what, in fact, his tiny pink-cheeked rotundity

suggested—an infant still. She found him adorable and unimportant. Even his sins—and in those days sins were serious—might, somehow or other, be disregarded; and besides, she observed that he had only one—it was *gaudeamus;* she scolded him with a smile. It was delightful to have anything to do with him—to talk with him, to laugh at him, to write to him. "Le style qu'on a en lui écrivant," she said, "ressemble à la joie et à la santé." It was true; and some of her most famous, some of her most delicious and life-scattering letters were written to her cousin Coulanges.

He married well—a lady who was related to the great Louvois; but the connection did him little good in the world. For a moment, indeed, an important public office was dangled before his eyes; but it was snapped up by somebody else, and Coulanges, after a few days of disappointment, consoled himself easily enough—with a song. He was very fond of songs, composing them with elegant rapidity to the popular airs of the day; every circumstance of his existence, however grave or however trivial—a journey, a joke, the world's cruelties, his wife's infidelities—he rigged them all out in the bows and ribbons of his little rhymes.

His wife was pretty, gay, fashionable, and noted for her epigrams. Her adorers were numerous: there was the Comte de Brancas, famous—immortal, even, as he has his niche in La Bruyère's gallery—for his absentmindedness; there was the Abbé Têtu, remarkable for two things—for remaining the friend both of Madame de Montespan and of Madame de Maintenon, and for being the first person who was ever afflicted by the vapours; and there was the victorious—the scandalously victorious—Marquis de la Trousse. Decidedly the lady was gay—too gay to be quite to the taste of Madame de Sévigné, who declared that she was a leaf fluttering in the wind. "Cette feuille," she said, "est la plus frivole et la plus légère marchandise que vous ayez jamais vue." But Coulanges was indifferent to her lightness; what he did feel was her inordinate success at Court. There she gadded, in a blaze of popularity, launching her epigrams and hobnobbing with Madame de Maintenon; he was out of it; and he was growing old, and the gout attacked him in horrid spasms. At times he was almost sad.

Then, gradually and for no apparent reason, there was a change. What was it? Was the world itself changing? Was one age going out and another coming in? From about the year 1690 onwards, one begins to discern the first signs of the petrifaction, the *rigor mortis* of the great epoch of Louis XIV; one begins to detect, more and more clearly in the circumambient atmosphere, the scent and savour of the eighteenth century. Already there had been symptoms—there had been the fairy *Cafut*, and the Abbé Têtu's vapours. But now there could be no more doubt about it; the new strange tide was flowing steadily in. And upon it was wafted the cockleshell of Coulanges. At fifty-seven, he found that he had come into his own. No longer was he out of it—far from it: his was now the popularity, the inordinate success. He was asked everywhere, and he always fitted in. His songs particularly, his frivolous neat little songs, became the rage; they flew from mouth to mouth; and the young people, at all the fashionable parties, danced as they sang them. At last they were collected by some busybody and printed, to his fury and delight; and his celebrity was redoubled. At the same time a wonderful rejuvenation came upon him; he seemed to grow younger daily; he drank, he guzzled, with astonishing impunity; there must have been a mistake, he said, in his birth certificate—it was antedated at least twenty years. As for his gout, it had gone for ever; he had drowned it by bathing, when he was over sixty, all one summer in the Seine. Madame de Sévigné could only be delighted. She had given a great deal of thought to the matter, she told him, and she had come to the conclusion that he was the happiest man in the world. Probably she was right—she almost always was. But, oddly enough, while Coulanges was undergoing this transformation, a precisely contrary one had befallen his wife. She had, in sober truth, grown old—old, and disillusioned, and serious. She could bear the Court no longer—she despised it; she wavered between piety and stoicism; quietly, persistently, she withdrew into herself. Madame de Sévigné, philosophizing and quoting La Fontaine, found—it was surprising—that she admired her—the poor brown leaf; and, on her side, Madame de Coulanges grew more and more devoted to Madame de Sévigné. Her husband mildly amused her. As she watched him flying from country-house to country-house, she suggested that it would save time and trouble if

55

he lived in a swing, so that he might whirl backwards and forwards for the rest of his days, without ever having to touch the earth again. "C'est toujours son plaisir qui le gouverne," she observed, with an ironical smile; "et il est heureux: en faut-il davantage?" Apparently not. Coulanges, adored by beautiful young Duchesses, disputed over by enormously wealthy Dowagers, had nothing left to wish for. The gorgeous Cardinal de Bouillon took him up—so did the Duc de Bouillon, and the Chevalier—all the Bouillons, in fact; it was a delightful family. The Cardinal carried him off to his country palace, where there was music all day long, and the servants had the air of noblemen, and the *ragouts* reached a height of ecstatic piquancy—*ragouts* from every country in Europe, it seemed—how they understood each other when they came together on his plate, he had no idea —but no matter; he ate them all.

In the midst of this, the inevitable and the unimaginable happened: Madame de Sévigné died. The source of order, light, and heat was no more; the reign of Chaos and Old Night descended. One catches a hurried vision of Madame de Grignan, pale as ashes, elaborating sentences of

grief; and then she herself and all her belongings
—her husband, her son, her castle, with its ter-
races and towers, its Canons, its violins, its Mis-
tral, its hundred guests—are utterly abolished.
For a little longer, through a dim penumbra,
Coulanges and his wife remain just visible. She
was struck down—overwhelmed with grief and
horror. Was it possible, was it really possible, that
Madame de Sévigné was dead? She could hardly
believe it. It was a reversal of nature. Surely it
could not be. She sat alone, considering life and
death, silent, harrowed, and sceptical, while her
husband—ah! even her husband felt this blow.
The little man wrote a piteous letter to Madame
de Grignan's daughter, young Madame de Simiane, and tears blotted the page. He was only a
shadow now—all too well he knew it; and yet
even shadows must obey the law of their being.
In a few weeks he wrote to Madame de Simiane
again; he was more cheerful; he was staying with
Madame de Louvois in her house at Choisy, a
truly delicious abode; but Madame de Simiane
must not imagine that he did not pass many moments, in spite of all the company, in sad remem-
brance of his friend. A few weeks more, and he

was dancing; the young people danced, and why should not he, who was as young as the youngest? All the Bouillons were in the house. The jigging vision grows fainter; but a few years later one sees him at the height of his felicity, having been provided by one of his kind friends with a room in the Palace at Versailles. More years pass, he is very old, he is very poor, but what does it matter?—

> Je connais de plus en plus
> En faisant très-grande chère,
> Qu'un estomac qui digère
> Vaut plus de cent mille écus.

On his seventy-sixth birthday he sings and dances, and looks forward to being a hundred without any difficulty at all. Then he eats and drinks, and sings and dances again. And so he disappears.

But Madame de Coulanges, ever sadder and more solitary, stayed in her room, thinking, hour after hour, over the fire. The world was nothing to her; success and happiness nothing; heaven itself nothing. She pulled her long fur-trimmed taffeta gown more closely round her, and pushed about the embers, wondering, for the thousandth time, whether it was really possible that Madame de Sévigné was dead.

The Sad Story of Dr. Colbatch

THE REV. DR. COLBATCH could not put up with
it any more. Animated by the highest motives, he felt that he must intervene. The task was
arduous, odious, dangerous; his antagonist most
redoubtable; but Dr. Colbatch was a Doctor of
Divinity, Professor of Casuistry in the University
of Cambridge, a Senior Fellow of Trinity College,
and his duty was plain; the conduct of the Master
could be tolerated no longer; Dr. Bentley must go.

In the early years of the eighteenth century the
life of learning was agitated, violent, and full of
extremes. Everything about it was on the grand
scale. Erudition was gigantic, controversies were
frenzied, careers were punctuated by brutal triumphs, wild temerities, and dreadful mortifica-
tions. One sat, bent nearly double, surrounded by
four circles of folios, living to edit Hesychius and
confound Dr. Hody, and dying at last with a
stomach half-full of sand. The very names of the
scholars of those days had something about them

at once terrifying and preposterous: there was
Graevius, there was Wolfius, there was Cruquius;
there were Torrentius and Rutgersius; there was
the gloomy Baron de Stosch, and there was the
deplorable De Pauw. But Richard Bentley was
greater than all these. Combining extraordinary
knowledge and almost infinite memory with an
acumen hardly to be distinguished from inspira-
tion, and a command of logical precision which
might have been envied by mathematicians or
generals in the field, he revivified with his daemonic energy the whole domain of classical scholarship. The peer of the mightiest of his predeces-
sors—of Scaliger, of Casaubon—turning, in skilful
strength, the magic glass of science, he brought
into focus the world's comprehension of ancient
literature with a luminous exactitude of which
they had never dreamed. His prowess had first
declared itself in his *Dissertation upon the Epistles of
Phalaris*, in which he had obliterated under cart-
loads of erudition and ridicule the miserable Mr.
Boyle. He had been rewarded, in the year 1700,
when he was not yet forty, with the Mastership of
Trinity; and then another side of his genius had
appeared. It became evident that he was not

merely a scholar, that he was a man of action and affairs, and that he intended to dominate over the magnificent foundation of Trinity with a command as absolute as that which he exercised over questions in Greek grammar. He had immediately gathered into his own hands the entire control of the College; he had manipulated the statutes, re-arranged the finances, packed the Council; he had compelled the Society to rebuild and redecorate, at great expense, his own Lodge; he had brought every kind of appointment—scholarships, fellow-ships, livings—to depend simply upon his will. The Fellows murmured and protested in vain; their terrible tyrant treated them with scant cere-mony. "You will die in your shoes!" he had shouted at one tottering Senior who had ven-tured to oppose him; and another fat and angry old gentleman he had named "The College Dog." In fact, he treated his opponents as if they had been corrupt readings in an old manuscript. At last there was open war. The leading Fellows had appealed to the Visitor of the College, the Bishop of Ely, to remove the Master; and the Master had replied by denying the Bishop's competence and declaring that the visitatorial power lay with the

Crown. His subtle mind had detected an ambiguity in the Charter; the legal position was, indeed, highly dubious; and for five years, amid indescribable animosities, he was able to hold his enemies at bay. In the meantime, he had not been idle in other directions: he had annihilated Le Clerc, who, ignorant of Greek, was rash enough to publish a Menander; he had produced a monumental edition of Horace; and he had pulverized Freethinking in the person of Anthony Collins. But his foes had pressed upon him; and eventually it had seemed that his hour was come. In 1714 he had been forced to appear before the Bishop's court; his defence had been weak; the Bishop had drawn up a judgment of deprivation. Then there had been a *coup de théâtre*. The Bishop had suddenly died before delivering judgment. All the previous proceedings lapsed, and Bentley ruled once more supreme in Trinity.

It was at this point that the Rev. Dr. Colbatch, animated by the highest motives, felt that he must intervene. Hitherto he had filled the *rôle* of a peacemaker; but now the outrageous proceedings of the triumphant Master—who, in the flush of victory, was beginning to expel hostile Fellows by force from the College, and had even refused to appoint Dr. Colbatch himself to the Vice-Mastership—called aloud for the resistance of every right-thinking man. And Dr. Colbatch flattered himself that he could resist to some purpose. He had devoted his life to the study of the law; he was a man of the world; he was acquainted with Lord Carteret; and he had written a book on Portugal. Accordingly, he hurried to London and interviewed great personages, who were all of them extremely sympathetic and polite; then he returned to Trinity, and, after delivering a fulminating sermon in the chapel, he bearded the Master at a College meeting, and actually had the nerve to answer him back. Just then, moreover, the tide seemed to be turning against the tyrant. Bentley, not content with the battle in his own College, had begun a campaign against the University. There was a hectic struggle, and then the Vice-Chancellor, by an unparalleled exercise of power, deprived Bentley of his degrees: the Master of Trinity College and the Regius Professor of Divinity was reduced to the status of an undergraduate. This delighted the heart of Dr. Colbatch. He flew to London, where Lord Carteret, as usual, was all smiles and agreement. When, a little later, the College living of Orewell fell vacant, Dr. Colbatch gave a signal proof of his power; for Bentley, after refusing to appoint him to the living, at last found himself obliged to give way. Dr. Colbatch entered the rectory in triumph; was it not clear that that villain at the Lodge was a sinking man? But, whether sinking or no, the villain could still use a pen to some purpose. In a pamphlet on a proposed edition of the New Testament, Bentley took occasion to fall upon Dr. Colbatch tooth and nail. The rector of Orewell was "a casuistic drudge," a "plodding pupil of Escobar," an insect, a snarling dog, a gnawing rat, a maggot, and a cabbage-head. His intellect was as dark as his countenance; his "eyes, muscles, and shoulders were wrought up into the most solemn posture of gravity"; he grinned horribly; he was probably mad; and his brother's beard was ludicrously long.

On this Dr. Colbatch, chattering with rage, brought an action against the Master for libel in the Court of the Vice-Chancellor. By a cunning legal device Bentley arranged that the action should be stopped by the Court of King's Bench.

Was it possible that Dr. Colbatch's knowledge of the law was not impeccable? He could not believe it, and forthwith composed a pamphlet entitled *Jus Academicum*, in which the whole case, in all its bearings, was laid before the public. The language of the pamphlet was temperate, the references to Bentley were not indecently severe; but, unfortunately, in one or two passages some expressions seemed to reflect upon the competence of the Court of King's Bench. The terrible Master saw his opportunity. He moved the Court of King's Bench to take cognizance of the *Jus Academicum* as a contempt of their jurisdiction. A cold shiver ran down Dr. Colbatch's spine. Was it conceivable? . . . But no! He had friends in London, powerful friends, who would never desert him. He rushed to Downing Street; Lord Townshend was reassuring; so was the Lord Chief Justice; and so was the Lord Chancellor. "Here," said Lord Carteret, waving a pen, "is the magician's wand that will always come to the rescue of Dr. Colbatch." Surely all was well. Nevertheless, he was summoned to appear before the Court of King's Bench in order to explain his pamphlet. The judge was old and testy; he misquoted Horace—"Jura negat sibi nata, nihil non abrogat"; "*Arrogat*, my lord!" said Dr. Colbatch. A little later the judge once more returned to the quotation, making the same error. "*Arrogat*, my lord!" cried Dr. Colbatch for the second time. Yet once again, in the course of his summing-up, the judge pronounced the word "abrogat"; "*Arrogat*, my lord!" screamed, for the third time, Dr. Colbatch. The interruption was fatal. The unhappy man was fined £50 and imprisoned for a week.

A less pertinacious spirit would have collapsed under such a dire misadventure; but Dr. Colbatch fought on. For ten years more, still animated by the highest motives, he struggled to dispossess the Master. Something was gained when yet another Bishop was appointed to the See of Ely—a Bishop who disapproved of Bentley's proceedings. With indefatigable zeal Dr. Colbatch laid the case before the Bishop of London, implored the Dean and Chapter of Westminster to interfere, and petitioned the Privy Council. In 1729 the Bishop of Ely summoned Bentley to appear before him; whereupon Bentley appealed to the Crown to decide who was the Visitor of Trinity College. For a moment Dr.

Colbatch dreamed of obtaining a special Act of Parliament to deal with his enemy; but even he shrank from such a desperate expedient; and at length, in 1732, the whole case came up for decision before the House of Lords. At that very moment Bentley published his edition of *Paradise Lost*, in which all the best passages were emended and rewritten—a book remarkable as a wild aberration of genius, and no less remarkable as containing, for the first time in print, "tow'ring o'er the alphabet like Saul," the great Digamma. If Bentley's object had been to impress his judges in his favour, he failed; for the House of Lords decided that the Bishop of Ely was the Visitor. Once more Bentley was summoned to Ely House. Dr. Colbatch was on tenterhooks; the blow was about to fall; nothing could avert it now, unless—he trembled—if the Bishop were to die again? But the Bishop did not die; in 1734 he pronounced judgment; he deposed Bentley.

So, after thirty years, a righteous doom had fallen upon that proud and wicked man. Dr. Colbatch's exultation was inordinate: it was only equalled, in fact, by his subsequent horror, indignation, and fury. For Bentley had discovered in

67

the Statutes of the College a clause which laid it down that, when the Master was to be removed, the necessary steps were to be taken by the Vice-Master. Now the Vice-Master was Bentley's creature; he never took the necessary steps; and Bentley never ceased, so long as he lived, to be Master of Trinity. Dr. Colbatch petitioned the House of Lords, he applied to the Court of King's Bench, he beseeched Lord Carteret—all in vain. His head turned; he was old, haggard, dying. Tossing on his bed at Orewell, he fell into a delirium; at first his mutterings were inarticulate; but suddenly, starting up, a glare in his eye, he exclaimed, with a strange emphasis, to the utter bewilderment of the bystanders, *"Arrogat,* my lord!" and immediately expired.

The Président de Brosses

A CHARMING and sometimes forgotten feature of the world as it used to be before the age of trains and telephones was the provincial capital. When Edinburgh was as far from London as Vienna is today, it was natural—it was inevitable —that it should be the centre of a local civilization, which, while it remained politically and linguistically British, developed a colour and a character of its own. In France there was the same pleasant phenomenon. Bordeau, Toulouse, Aix-en-Provence—up to the end of the eighteenth century each of these was in truth a capital, where a peculiar culture had grown up that was at once French and idiosyncratic. An impossibility today! It is hard to believe, as one whisks through Dijon in a tram, that here, a hundred and fifty years ago, was the centre of a distinct and vigorous civilization—until, perhaps, one leaves the tram, and turns aside into the rue de la Préfecture. Ah! One has come upon a vanished age. The houses, so solid and yet so vivacious, with their cobbled courts and coloured tiles, seem to be withdrawn into an aristocratic resignation. Memory and forgetfulness are everywhere. It is the moment to reflect upon the Président de Brosses.

Dijon, the capital of Burgundy, had become in the eighteenth century pre-eminently a city of magistrates. There the provincial *parlement* assembled and the laws were administered by the hereditary judges, the nobility of the long robe, whose rule was more immediate, more impressive, and almost more powerful, than the King's. Charles de Brosses was born into this aristocracy, and grew up to be a perfect representative of its highest traditions. He was extremely intelligent, admirably conscientious, and crammed full of life. He was at once a wit, a scholar, a lawyer, and a man of the world. He resembled the generous wine of the country in his combination of gay vitality with richness and strength. His tiny figure and his satirical face lost in the forest of a judicial wig might prompt to laughter—"the corners of one's mouth," said Diderot, "couldn't help going up when one looked at him"; but he was impressive on the bench; and, late in life, was to prove his patriotism by his intrepid resistance when the privileges of his province were attacked by the royal authority. In his leisure, he devoted himself to every kind of literary and scientific work. A tour in Italy produced a series of amusing letters, which, published posthumously, are still read and remembered; his book on the newly discovered Herculaneum (1750) was the first on the subject; his *Histoire des navigations des Terres Australes* (1756) was of use to both Cook and Bougainville; his *Culte des Dieux Fétiches* (1760) contained a curious speculation on the origin of the religion of Egypt; his *Traité de la formation mécanique des langues* (1765) was the earliest attempt at a science of etymology; and his labours were concluded with an elaborate edition of *Sallust* (1777) upon which he had worked for thirty years. The growth of knowledge has converted his researches and his speculations into mere curiosities; but it was natural that the citizens of Dijon should have honoured him as one of their most splendid luminaries, and that the Président de Brosses should have been compared in his day to that other great provincial figure of a previous generation—the Président de Montesquieu. Of course, though Dijon was select and

Dijon was magnificent, it had to be admitted that there did exist a higher tribunal, at whose bar taste, learning, and behaviour received their final doom or their crowning approbation: the drawing-rooms of Paris reigned supreme. In those drawing-rooms the Président was well thought of; he had powerful friends at Court; was it not to be expected that at last, in the fullness of time, his worth would be completely recognized and receive its due reward in the highest honour that could fall to a man of his pretensions—a seat in the Academy? A prize, indeed, that it was impossible not to hope for! The promises of other worlds had grown dim and dubious; but here, among the glorious forty, was a definite, and indisputable immortality—and one, moreover, that possessed the singular advantage of being enjoyable here and now, while the eighteenth-century sun still shone on the rue de la Préfecture.

The Président was at the height of his exuberant manhood—he was not yet fifty—when something occurred which had a strange and unexpected effect upon his history. Voltaire, having quarrelled with Frederick the Great and shaken the dust of Potsdam from his feet, had been wandering for some years in uncertainty among the minor states that lay between France and Germany. He had settled for a time at Colmar; he had moved to Lausanne; then he had gone to Geneva and taken a country house in its neighbourhood. But the Calvinism of the townspeople, who frowned at his passion for private theatricals, annoyed him; and his eye fell on the house and territory of Ferney, which was just inside the borders of France, but, lying on the eastern slopes of the Jura mountains, was so remote as to be almost independent of French control and within a drive of the free city of Geneva. This was exactly what he wanted—a secluded abode, where he would have elbow-room for his activities, and from which he could bolt at any moment, if things became too hot for him. Accordingly, in 1758, he bought Ferney, where he lived for the rest of his life; and at the same time he entered into negotiations for the purchase of a neighbouring property—that of Tournay—which belonged to the Président de Brosses. The Président, who already had a slight acquaintance with the great man— his wife, a Crévecœur, was the daughter of one of Voltaire's oldest friends—declared that he would be delighted to oblige him. There was some stiff haggling, for each party prided himself on his business capacity, but eventually Voltaire, for 35,000 francs, became possessed of the domain of Tournay—which included the right to the title of Count—on a life-tenancy. The bargain, obviously, was something of a gamble; the new Comte de Tournay was sixty-four, and, so he declared, on the point of death; but then he had been on the point of death ever since any one could remember. When it was all over, the Président had an uneasy feeling that he had been done. The feeling increased as time went on, and his agent informed him that the estate was being allowed to go to rack and ruin. He complained; but the poet replied with a flat denial, declared—what was quite true—that he had built a theatre at Tournay, and begged the Président to come and see his latest tragedy performed in it. A little later, a new manoeuvre began: Voltaire proposed that he should buy the property outright. The Président was not altogether averse; but this time he was far more cautious; as the negotiations proceeded, he became privately convinced that an attempt was being made to cheat him; but he said nothing, and the proposal lapsed. Voltaire, on his side, was none too pleased with his bargain. The land of Tournay was poor, and the Countship had brought with it various responsibilities and expenses not at all to his taste. He was vexed; and his vexation took the form of bothering the Président, in letter after letter, with a multitude of legal questions upon points connected with the property. The Président was also vexed; but he answered every letter and every question with extreme civility.

In this way two years passed—two years during which the Président published his *Culte des Dieux Fétiches* and Voltaire his *Candide*. The old creature at Ferney was at last beginning to settle down to the final and by far the most important period of his immense and extraordinary career. Free, rich, happy, with his colossal reputation and his terrific energy, he was starting on the great adventure of his life—his onslaught upon Christianity. Meanwhile his vitality and his pugnacity were satisfying themselves in a multitude of minor ways. He was belabouring Rousseau, tortuing Fréron, annihilating le Franc de Pompignan; he was corresponding with all the world, he was composing half a

75

dozen tragedies, he was writing the life of Peter the Great, he was preparing a monumental edition of Corneille. When, in the midst of these and a hundred other activities, he received a bill for 281 francs from a peasant called Charlot Baudy for fourteen loads of wood from Tournay, he brushed the matter on one side. More bother from Tournay! But it was ridiculous—why should he pay for wood from his own estate? And besides, he remembered quite well that the Président, before the sale was completed, had told him that he could have as much wood as he wanted. He did nothing, and when Charlot Baudy pressed for the money, refused to pay. Then, early in 1761, a letter arrived from the Président. "Agréez, Monsieur," he began, "que je vous demande l'explication d'une chose tout-à-fait singulière." Charlot Baudy, he continued, had, *before the sale of Tournay*, bought from the Président the cut wood on the estate; Baudy had now sent in his account of what he owed the Président, and had subtracted from it the sum of 281 francs for wood supplied to M. de Voltaire; his reason for this was that M. de Voltaire had told him that the wood was a gift from the Président. "Je vous demande excuse," the letter went on, "si je vous répète un tel propos: car vous sentez bien que je suis fort éloigné de croire que vous l'ayez tenu, et je n'y ajoute pas la moindre foi. Je ne prends ceci que pour le discours d'un homme rustique fait pour ignorer les usages du monde et les convenances; qui ne sait pas qu'on envoie bien à son ami et son voisin un panier de pêches, mais que si on s'avisait de lui faire la galanterie de quatorze moules de bois, il le prendrait pour une absurdité contraire aux bienséances." The sarcasm was clear and cutting, and the Président proceeded to give his own account of what had occurred. He distinctly remembered, he said, that Voltaire, at the time of the negotiations about Tournay, had in the course of conversation complained of a lack of firewood, and that he had thereupon recommended Baudy as the man who would supply Voltaire with as much as he wanted. That was all; the offensive notion of a present had never entered his head. "J'espère," he concluded, "que vous voudrez bien faire incontinent payer cette bagatelle à Charlot, parce que, comme je me ferai certainement payer de lui, il aurait infailliblement aussi son recours contre vous; ce qui ferait une affaire du genre de celles qu'un homme tel que vous ne veut point avoir."

It was obvious to any one in his senses that the Président was right: that his account of the matter was the true one, and that, as he had said, the only reasonable thing for Voltaire to do was to pay Baudy the money—the miserable sum of money!—and finish the business. But Voltaire was not in his senses—he never was when even the most miserable sum of money was concerned. He could not bear to think of parting with 281 francs. It was monstrous; the land and everything on it was his; the wood had been given him; he would not be set down; and this wretched man had dared to be ironical! At any rate, he had had the wood and burnt it, and the Président de Brosses might do what he liked. Accordingly, in his next letter, he airily dismissed the subject. "It is no longer a question," he said, "of Charles Baudy and four loads of wood"—and proceeded to discuss an entirely different matter. The Président replied in detail, and then reverted for a moment to Baudy—"Four loads—read *fourteen;* you dropped a figure; we call this a *lapsus linguae*"; —and he begged Voltaire once more to avoid the painful publicity of a lawsuit. Voltaire made no reply; he hoped the whole thing was over; but he was wrong. In June, the Président sued Baudy for 281 francs, and in July Baudy sued Voltaire for the same sum. The cases came on at the local court, and were adjourned.

And now the fury of the frantic old desperado flamed up sky-high. Seizing his pen, he poured out, in letter after letter to all the lawyers in Dijon, his account of what had happened—the swindling to which he had been subjected—the insults to which he had been exposed. To a particular friend, the Président de Ruffey, he sent a long formal statement of his case, followed by a private sheet of enraged argumentation. As for his enemy, he was no longer a président—the little bewigged monster—he was a fetish. He would see to it that the nickname stuck. "Le Fétiche," he shrieked, "demande de l'argent de ses moules et de ses fagots. . . . Le misérable m'accable d'exploits." He had put up Baudy, who was a man of straw, to do his dirty work. "Songez qu'il faisait cette infâmie dans le temps qu'il recevait de moi 47 mille livres! . . . Qu'il tremble! Il ne s'agit pas de le rendre ridicule: il s'agit de le déshonorer."

Cela m'afflige. Mais il payera cher la bassesse d'un procéde si coupable et si lache." Finally he addressed the Fetish himself in a letter composed in his most magnificent style. "Vous n'êtes donc venu chez moi, Monsieur, vous ne m'avez offert votre amitié, que pour empoisonner par des procès la fin de ma vie." In great detail he went over the whole dispute. With singular violence, and no less singular obtuseness, he asserted the hopelessly contradictory propositions, both that the wood was his own and that the Président had given it him; hc hinted that his enemy would make use of his position to pervert the course of justice; and he ended with threats. "S'il faut que M. le Chancelier, et les Ministres, et tout Paris, soient instruits de votre procédé, ils le seront; et, s'il se trouve dans votre Compagnie respectable une personne qui vous approuve, je me condamne."

The Président's moment had come—the testing moment of his life. What was he to do? It was still not too late to withdraw, to pay the money with a shrug of the shoulders and put an end to this fearful hubbub and this terrifying enmity. For a short space, he wavered. It was true that

Voltaire was the greatest writer of the age, and perhaps he deserved some allowances on that score. In any case, he was an extremely dangerous antagonist—a man who had made mincemeat of all his literary opponents and fought on equal terms with Frederick the Great. But no! It was intolerable! His Burgundian blood boiled, and the proud traditions of aristocracy and the judicial habits of a lifetime asserted themselves. "Là-dessus on dit":—so he explained later to a friend —"c'est un homme dangereux. Et à cause de cela, faut-il donc le laisser être méchant impunément? Ce sont au contraire ces sortes de gens-là qu'il faut châtier. Je ne le crains pas. . . . On l'admire, parce qu'il fait d'excellents vers. Sans doute il les fait excellents. Mais ce sont ses vers qu'il faut admirer." And so, taking Voltaire's letter, he wrote upon the margin of it a reply, in which he not only rebutted his arguments but told him exactly what he thought of him. Point by point he exposed the futility of Voltaire's contentions. He showed that there was actually a clause in the lease, by which the cut wood on the estate was specifically excepted from the sale. He offered to drop the matter if Voltaire would send him a receipt in the following terms: "Je soussigné, François-Marie Arouet de Voltaire, chevalier, seigneur de Ferney, gentilhomme ordinaire de la chambre du Roi, reconnois que M. de Brosses, président du Parlement, m'a fait présent de . . . voies de bois de moule, pour mon chauffage, en valeur de 281 f., dont je le remercie." He pointed out that otherwise he had nothing to do with the business, that Voltaire owed the money to Charlot Baudy, and that it was indeed extraordinary to see "un homme si riche et si illustre se tourmenter à tel excès pour ne pas payer à un paysan 280 livres pour du bois de chauffage qu'il a fourni." His incidental remarks were nothing if not outspoken. "En vérité," he wrote, "je gémis pour l'humanité de voir un si grand génie avec un cœur si petit sans cesse tiraillé par des misères de jalousie et de lésine. C'est vous-même qui empoisonnez une vie si bien faite d'ailleurs pour être heureuse." As for the suggestion that he would bring undue influence to bear upon the case,—"il ne convient pas de parler ainsi: soyez assez sage à l'avenir pour ne rien dire de pareil à un magistrat." "Tenez vous pour dit," the letter concluded, "de ne m'écrire plus ni sur cette matière ni surtout de ce ton. Je vous fais, Monsieur, le souhait de Perse: *Mens sana in corpore sano.*"

It is difficult indeed to imagine the scene at Ferney while Voltaire was deciphering, on the edges of his own letter, this devastating reply. But there was worse to follow. A note came from the Président de Ruffey, in which, with infinite politeness, he made it clear that in his opinion Voltaire had no case, and that he had better pay. At the same time Ruffey wrote to Madame Denis, Voltaire's niece, advising her to give the money privately to Baudy. Madame Denis had not the courage to do so; she showed the letter to her uncle, who, in a dictated reply, still tried to keep up an appearance of self-confidence. "Je ne crains point les Fétiches," he added in his own hand. "Et les Fétiches doivent me craindre." And again, at the bottom of the paper, he scribbled, "N.B. Il n'y a qu'une voix sur le Fétiche." But such screams were useless; the game was up. The Président's letter remained unanswered; Voltaire swallowed in silence the incredible affront; and when, a little later, the Président, feeling that he could afford to be magnanimous, informed a common friend that he would cancel his account with Baudy if Voltaire gave 281 francs to the poor of Tournay, the great man was glad enough to fall in with the suggestion.

The Président had triumphed; but could he really have supposed that he would escape from such an antagonist unscathed? The sequel came ten years later, when the Président Hénault died and left a seat vacant at the Academy. There was a strong movement in favour of electing the Président de Brosses. There appeared to be no other very suitable candidate; his friends rallied round him; and D'Alembert, writing to Voltaire from Paris, assured him that there was every likelihood that "ce plat Président" would be chosen for the vacant place. The serious feature of the case was that the old Maréchal de Richelieu, who, after a lifetime of fighting and gallantry, amused his decrepitude by making his influence felt in affairs of this kind, supported him. What was to be done? Voltaire was equal to the occasion: his letters flew. At all costs the Fetish must be kept out. He wrote repeatedly to Richelieu, in that tone of delicate cajolery of which he was a master, touching upon their ancient friendship, and spinning a strange tale of the perfidies committed by "ce

84

petit persécuteur nasilloneur," until the Maréchal melted, and promised to withdraw his support. Finally Voltaire despatched to D'Alembert a signed declaration to the effect that he would himself resign from the academy if Brosses was elected. This settled the matter, and no more was heard of the candidature of the Président. It seems likely that he never knew what it was that had baulked him of the ambition of his life. For 281 francs he had lost the immortality of the Academy. A bad bargain, no doubt; and yet, after all, the transaction had gained him another, and in fact a unique, distinction: he would go down to history as the man who had got the better of Voltaire.

James Boswell

IT WOULD be difficult to find a more shattering refutation of the lessons of cheap morality than the life of James Boswell. One of the most extraordinary successes in the history of civilization was achieved by an idler, a lecher, a drunkard, and a snob. Nor was this success of that sudden explosive kind which is frequent enough with youthful genius—the inspired efflorescence of a Rimbaud or a Swinburne; it was essentially the product of long years of accumulated energy; it was the supreme expression of an entire life. Boswell triumphed by dint of abandoning himself, through fifty years, to his instincts. The example, no doubt, is not one to be followed rashly. Self-indulgence is common, and Boswells are rare. The precise character of the rarity we are now able, for the first time, to estimate with something like completeness. Boswell's nature and inner history cannot be fully understood from the works published by himself. It is only in his letters that the whole man is revealed. Professor Tinker, by collecting together Boswell's correspondence and editing it with scholarly exactitude, has done a great service to English literature.[1] There is, in fact, only one fault to be found with this admirable book. Professor Tinker shows us more of Boswell than any previous editor, but he does not show us all that he might. Like the editors of Walpole's Letters and Pepys's Diary, while giving himself credit for rehabilitating the text of his author, he admits in the same breath that he has mutilated it. When will this silly and barbarous prudery come to an end?

Boswell's career was completely dominated by his innate characteristics. Where they came from it is impossible to guess. He was the strangest sport: the descendant of Scotch barons and country gentlemen, the son of a sharp lowland lawyer, was an artist, a spendthrift, a buffoon, with a passion for literature, and without any dignity whatever. So he was born, and so he remained; life taught him nothing—he had nothing to learn; his course was marked out, immutably, from the

[1] "Letters of James Boswell." Collected and edited by Chauncey Brewster Tinker. 2 vols. (Oxford: Clarendon Press.)

87

beginning. At the age of twenty-three he discovered Dr. Johnson. A year later he was writing to him, at Wittenberg, "from the tomb of Melanchthon": "My paper rests upon the gravestone of that great and good man. . . . At this tomb, then, my ever dear and respected friend! I vow to thee an eternal attachment." The rest of Boswell's existence was the history of that vow's accomplishment. But his connection with Dr. Johnson was itself only the crowning instance of an overwhelming predisposition, which showed itself in a multitude of varied forms. There were other great men, for instance—there was Mr. Wilkes, and General Paoli, and Sir David Dalrymple. One of Professor Tinker's most delightful discoveries is a series of letters from the youthful Boswell to Jean-Jacques Rousseau, in which all the writer's most persistent qualities—his literary skill, his psychological perspicacity, his passion for personalities, and his amazing aptitude for self-revelation—are exquisitely displayed. "Dites-moi," he asked the misanthropic sentimentalist, "ne ferai-je bien de m'appliquer véritablement à la musique, jusque à un certain point? Dites-moi quel doit être mon instrument. C'est tard je l'avoue. Mais n'aurai-je le plaisir de faire un progrès continuel, et ne serai-je pas capable d'adoucir ma vieillesse par les sons de ma lyre?" Rousseau was completely melted. The elder Pitt, however, was made of sterner stuff. When Boswell appeared before him in the costume of a Corsican chieftain, "Lord Chatham," we are told, "smiled, but received him very graciously in his Pompous manner"— and there the acquaintance ended; in spite of Boswell's modest suggestion that the Prime Minister should "honour me now and then with a letter. . . . To correspond with a Paoli and with a Chatham is enough to keep a young man ever ardent in the pursuit of virtuous fame."

Fame—though perhaps it was hardly virtuous —Boswell certainly attained; but his ardent pursuit of it followed the track of an extraordinary zigzag which could never have had anything in common with letters from Lord Chatham. His own letters to his friend Temple lay bare the whole unique peregrination, from start to finish. To confess is the desire of many; but it is within the power of few. A rare clarity of vision, a still rarer candour of expression—without these qualities it is vain for a man to seek to unburden his heart. Boswell possessed them in the highest degree; and, at the same time, he was untroubled by certain other qualities, which, admirable though they be in other connections, are fatal for this particular purpose. He had no pride, no shame, and no dignity. The result was that a multitude of inhibitions passed him by. Nevertheless he was by no means detached. His was not the method of the scientific observer, noting his introspections with a cold exactness—far from it; he was intimately fascinated by everything to do with himself—his thoughts, his feelings, his reactions; and yet he was able to give expression to them all with absolute ingenuousness, without a shade of self-consciousness, without a particle of reserve. Naturally enough the picture presented in such circumstances is full of absurdities, for no character which had suppressed its absurdities could possibly depict itself so. Boswell was *ex hypothesi* absurd: it was his absurdity that was the essential condition of his consummate art.

It was in the description of his love affairs that this truly marvellous capacity found its fullest scope. The succession of his passions, with all their details, their variations, their agitations, and

their preposterousnesses, fill the letters to Temple
(a quiet clergyman in the depths of Devonshire)
with a constant effervescence of delight. One pro-
gresses with marvellous exhilaration from Miss
W——t ("just such a young lady as I could wish
for the partner of my soul") to Zelide ("upon my
soul, Temple, I must have her"), and so to the
Signora, and the Moffat woman ("can I do better
than keep a dear infidel for my hours of Paphian
bliss?"), and the Princess ("here every flower is
united"), and the gardener's daughter, and Mrs.
D., and Miss Bosville, and La Belle Irlandaise
("just sixteen, formed like a Grecian nymph, with
the sweetest countenance, full of sensibility, accomplished, with a Dublin education"), and Mrs.
Boswell ("I am fully sensible of my happiness in
being married to so excellent a woman"), and
Miss Silverton ("in the fly with me, an amiable
creature who has been in France. I can unite
little fondnesses with perfect conjugal love"), and
Miss Bagnal ("*a Ranelagh girl*, but of excellent
principles, in so much that she reads prayers to
the servants in her father's family, every Sunday
evening. 'Let me see such a woman,' cried I"),
and Miss Milles ("*d'une certaine âge*, and with a

91

fortune of £10,000"), and—but the catalogue is endless. These are the pages which record the sunny hours of Boswell's chequered day. Light and warmth sparkle from them; but, even in the noon of his happiness, there were sudden clouds. Hypochondria seized him; he would wake in the night "dreading annihilation, or being thrown into some horrible state of being." His conscience would not leave him alone; he was attacked by disgraceful illnesses; he felt "like a man ordered for ignominious execution"; he feared that his infidelities to Mrs. Boswell would not be excused hereafter. And then his vital spirits rushed to his rescue, and the shadow fled. Was he not the friend of Paoli? Indeed he was; and he was sitting in a library forty feet long, dressed in green and gold. The future was radiant. "My warm imagination looks forward with great complacency on the sobriety, the healthfulness, and the worth of my future life." As for his infidelities, were they so reprehensible after all? "Concubinage is almost universal. If it was *morally* wrong, why was it permitted to the pious men under the Old Testament? Why did our Saviour never say a word against it?"

As his life went on, however, the clouds grew

thicker and more menacing, and the end was storm and darkness. The climax came with the death of his wife. Boswell found himself at the age of fifty alone in the world with embarrassed fortunes, a family of young children to bring up, and no sign that any of the "towering hopes" of his youth had been realized. Worse still, he had become by this time a confirmed drunkard. His self-reproaches were pitiable; his efforts at amendment never ceased; he took a vow of sobriety under "a venerable yew"; he swore a solemn oath that he would give up drinking altogether—that he would limit himself to four glasses of wine at dinner and a pint afterwards; but it was all in vain. His way of life grew more and more disorderly, humiliating, and miserable. If he had retired to Scotland, and lived economically on his estate, he might have retrieved his position; but that was what he could not do; he could not be out of London. His ambitions seemed to multiply with his misfortunes. He exchanged the Scotch bar for the English, and lost all his professional income at a blow. He had wild hopes of becoming a Member of Parliament, if only he toadied Lord Lonsdale sufficiently; and Lord Lonsdale promised much, asked him to his castle, made a butt of him, hid his wig, was gravely concerned, and finally threw him off after "expressing himself in the most degrading manner in presence of a low man from Carlisle and one of his menial servants." Consolations now were few indeed. It was something, no doubt, to be able to go to Court. "I was the *great man* at the late drawing-room in a suit of imperial blue lined with rose-coloured silk, and ornamented with rich gold-wrought buttons. What a motley scene is life!" And at Eton, where he was "carried to dine at the Fellows' table," it was pleasant enough to find that in spite of a Scotch education one could still make a creditable figure. "I had my classical quotations very ready." But these were fleeting gleams. "Your kindness to me," he burst out to Temple, in April, 1791, "fairly makes me shed tears. Alas, I fear that my constitutional melancholy, which returns in such dismal fits and is now aggravated by the loss of my valuable wife, must prevent me from any permanent felicity in this life. I snatch *gratifications;* but have no *comfort*, at least very little. . . . I get bad rest in the night, and then I brood over all my complaints—the *sickly mind* which I have had

94

from my early years—the disappointment of my hopes of success in life—the irrevocable separation between me and that excellent woman who was my cousin, my friend, and my wife—the embarrassment of my affairs—the disadvantage to my children in having so wretched a father—nay, the want of *absolute certainty* of being happy after death, the *sure prospect* of which is *frightful*. No more of this."

The tragedy was closing; but it was only superficially a sordid one. Six weeks later the writer of these lines published, in two volumes quarto, the *Life of Dr. Johnson*. In reality, Boswell's spirit had never failed. With incredible persistence he had carried through the enormous task which he had set himself thirty years earlier. Everything else was gone. He was burnt down to the wick, but his work was there. It was the work of one whose appetite for life was insatiable—so insatiable that it proved in the end self-destructive. The same force which produced the *Life of Johnson* plunged its author into ruin and desperation. If Boswell had been capable of retiring to the country and economizing we should never have heard of him. It was Lord Lonsdale's butt who reached immortality.

95

The Abbé Morellet

TALLEYRAND once remarked that only those who had lived in France before the Revolution had really experienced *la douceur de vivre*. The Abbé Morellet would have agreed with him. Born in 1727 at Lyons, the son of a small paper merchant, how was it possible, in that age of caste and privilege, that André Morellet should have known anything of life but what was hard, dull, and insignificant? So one might have supposed; but the contrary was the case. Before he was thirty this young man, without either fortune or connections, and without taking very much trouble about it, found himself a member of the most brilliant society in Paris, the close friend of the famous and the great, with a rosy future before him. The secret of it was simple: he had shown that he was intelligent; and in those days a little intelligence went a long way. So, indeed, did a little—a very little—money. A thousand francs from a generous cousin had opened Paris to him, by enabling him to go to the Sorbonne, whence, after five years, he had emerged an Abbé and an infidel. A chance meeting with Diderot did the rest. The great *philosophe*, forty years of age and at the height of his intellectual power, completely captivated a youth whose eager mind was only waiting for new ideas and new activities. Every Sunday morning the Abbé scaled the stairs to Diderot's lodging, to sit entranced for hours, while the Master poured forth the irresistible floods of his amazing conversation. "J'ai éprouvé peu de plaisirs de l'esprit au-dessus de celui-là," wrote Morellet long afterwards; "et je m'en souviendrai toujours." One can well believe it. The young man listened so intelligently that Diderot soon saw he would do; enrolled him among his disciples; introduced him to all his friends; and set him to write articles for his great Encyclopaedia. *La douceur de vivre* had begun.

Thirty delightful years followed—years of exciting work, delicious friendship, and ever-growing optimism. The great battle for liberty, tolerance, reason, and humanity was in full swing; the forces of darkness were yielding more and more rapidly; and Morellet was in the forefront of the fight. He wrote with untiring zeal. Besides his Encyclopaedia articles, he produced pamphlets in favour of the Protestants, he brought out a *Manuel des Inquisiteurs* exposing the methods of the Inquisition, he translated Beccaria's great work. But his principal interest was political economy. A close friend of Turgot, he was one of the earliest believers in Free Trade. He translated *The Wealth of Nations;* though the cast of his mind contrasted curiously with Adam Smith's. The Abbé, like most of the *philosophes,* preferred the *a priori* mode of argument. The reasons which led him to favour Free Trade are characteristic. The rights of property, he argued, are fundamental to the very existence of civilized society; now to interfere with the freedom of exchange is to attack one of the rights of property; therefore Protection and civilization are incompatible. This extremely complete argument seems to have escaped the notice of Tory Free Traders.

But the Abbé was not merely enlightened and argumentative; he had another quality which was essential in those days if one was to make any figure at all: he was malicious—though only, of course, at the expense of "the enemies of reason."

Some particularly biting little fly-sheets of his actually brought a word of praise from the mighty Patriarch of Ferney. "Embrassez pour moi l'Abbé Mords-les," wrote Voltaire to a common friend; "je ne connais personne qui soit plus capable de rendre service à la raison." This was a testimonial indeed! Morellet's reputation went up with a bound, and he himself declared that the sentence was all he wanted by way of an epitaph.

Only one thing more was needed to make his success complete; and that a kindly fate provided. Palissot, a *protégé* of a certain great lady, the Princesse de Robecq, attacked the *philosophes* in a satirical farce. Morellet, among the rest, replied with a stinging pamphlet; but he was unwise enough to direct some of his sharp remarks, not at Palissot, but at the Princess. This could not be allowed. Madame de Robecq had been the mistress of the Duc de Choiseul, who was all-powerful with Madame de Pompadour and, through her, with the King. A *lettre de cachet* sent Morellet to the Bastille. One can imagine no more striking example of the corruption and tyranny of the *ancien régime*—if only the poor Abbé had been treated properly—thrown into an underground dungeon, let us say, loaded with chains, and fed on bread and water. Unfortunately, nothing of the sort occurred. The victim was given a comfortable room, plenty of excellent food, a bottle of wine a day, provided with writing materials, and allowed all the books he asked for, besides being given the run of the Bastille library, which was especially strong in novels. He spent three months in peaceful study; and returned to liberty with the added glory of martyrdom.

Liberty and martyrdom—one hardly knew which was the pleasanter. In Paris one's mornings passed in reading and writing—the quill dashing over the paper with a heavenly speed; and one's afternoons and evenings were spent in company. There were dinners at D'Holbach's; there were the nightly gatherings in the little rooms of Mademoiselle de Lespinasse; there were lunches with Madame Geoffrin; and everywhere and always the conversation was copious and audacious to an intoxicating degree. Madame Geoffrin, indeed, insisted upon limits. "Voilà qui est bien!" she used to exclaim, when the talk grew too wild and high. Then the more reckless spirits, headed by D'Alembert, would go out into the Tuileries Gardens, and, sitting under the trees, continue the discourse until the exploded ruins of religions, philosophies, and conventions fell in showers about their ears. If Paris grew too hot or too noisy, there was always, close at hand, Auteuil. There lived Madame Helvétius, the widow of one of the leading *philosophes*, in a charming little villa, with a garden and all the simple pleasures of a country life. A curious *ménage*, highly typical of the nation and the age, was gathered together between those friendly walls. Morellet spent every summer and all his week-ends there; another clever Abbé also had rooms in the house; and so had a younger man, Cabanis, to whom Madame Helvétius was particularly attached. The elements of sentiment and friendship were so perfectly balanced between the four that their harmony and happiness were complete. Year after year the summers waxed and waned in the Auteuil garden, while Morellet lingered there, with peace, wit, kindness, and beauty around him. What was there left to wish for? Well! it would be nice, he sometimes thought, to have a little—a very little— more money. His income—made up of a few small pensions and legacies—was about £100 a year.

A most pleasant interlude was a visit to England, where Morellet spent several months as the guest of Lord Shelburne. Shelburne was a failure at politics (he was a Prime Minister and a man of intellect—a hazardous combination); but he made an admirable host. Garrick and Franklin were asked down to Bowood to meet the Abbé, and then he was carried off on a driving tour all over England. One day, near Plymouth, there was a picnic on the banks of the Tamar. After the meal, as the company lay on the grass, and the evening fell, three country girls made their appearance; on which the Abbé, offering them a basket of cherries, asked them, in his broken English, for a song. They smiled, and blushed; but sing they did, in unison, with the sweetest voices. The description of the scene in Morellet's *Mémoires* reads like a page from the *Vicar of Wakefield*.

Even affluence came at last. The incumbent of a priory, the reversion of which had been given to Morellet by Turgot twenty years before, died, and the Abbé found himself in the possession of a spacious country house, with land, and an income of £600 a year. This was in 1788. In less than a year all was over. The Abbé never lived in his priory. The tempest of the Revolution engulfed both him and it. The rights of property were violated, and the priest was deprived of a sinecure that he was enjoying as a member of a Church in which he disbelieved. Morellet's surprised indignation at this catastrophe—his absolute unconsciousness that the whole effort of his life had been in reality directed towards this very goal—makes comic reading—comic, and pathetic too. For still worse was to follow. The happy *ménage* at Auteuil was broken up. Cabanis and the other Abbé believed in the Revolution; Madame Helvétius agreed with them; and Morellet, finding himself in a minority of one, after a violent scene left the villa for ever. His plight was serious; but he weathered the storm. A revolutionary tribunal, before which he was haled, treated him gently, partly because it transpired in the course of the proceedings that he had been a friend of Turgot, "*ce bon citoyen*"; he was dismissed with a caution. Then, besides saving his own neck, he was able to do a good turn to the *Académie Française*, of which he was the Director. When that body was broken up, the care of its valuable possessions—its papers and its portraits—fell to him.

He concealed everything in various hiding-places, from which he drew forth the precious relics in triumph, when the days of order returned.

For they did return; and the Abbé, very old and very tired, found his way, with one or two others, to young Madame de Rémusat's drawing-room. There he sat dozing by the fire, while the talk sped on around him; dozing, and nodding; then suddenly waking up to denounce Monsieur de Châteaubriand and lament the ruin of French prose. He was treated with great respect by everybody; even the First Consul was flattering; even the Emperor was polite, and made him a Senator. Then the Emperor vanished, and a Bourbon ruled once more on the throne of his fathers. With that tenacity of life which seems to have been the portion of the creatures of the eighteenth century, Morellet continued in this world until his ninety-second year. But this world was no longer what it used to be: something had gone wrong. Those agitations, those arrangements and rearrangements, they seemed hardly worth attending to. One might as well doze. All his young friends were very kind certainly, but did they understand? How could they? What had been their ex-

perience of life? As for him, ah! *he* had listened to
Diderot—used to sit for hours talking in the
Tuileries Gardens with D'Alembert and Mademoiselle de Lespinasse—mentioned by Voltaire—
spent half a lifetime at Auteuil with dear Madame
Helvétius—imprisoned in the Bastille . . . he
nodded. Yes! *He* had known *la douceur de vivre.*

Mary Berry

" Amor, che a nullo amato amar perdona":
there could be no better summary of the
tragic romance of Madame du Deffand, Horace
Walpole, and Mary Berry. For Love moves in a
mysterious way, and the Paolos and Francescas
of this world, though they may be the most attractive of his victims, are not the most remarkable. Madame du Deffand was blind and nearly
seventy when, after a long career of brilliant dissipation and icy cynicism, she was suddenly overwhelmed by a passion which completely dominated her existence, until she died, fifteen years
later, at the age of eighty-three. Horace Walpole,
the object of this extraordinary adoration, was a
middle-aged man of fashion, a dilettante, whose
heart, like hers, had never felt a violent emotion,
and, naturally enough, was not induced to do so
by this strange catastrophe. He was flattered, he
was charmed; but he was obsessed by a terror of
ridicule; his enemies—worse still, his friends—

would laugh if they ever got wind of this romantic aberration; and so he mixed kindness and severity, ruthlessness and attentions, in so fatally medicinal a potion that the unhappy creature in Paris died at last less of old age than a broken heart. But "the whirligig of Time brings in his revenges." Walpole himself, when he was over seventy, suffered the same fate as Madame du Deffand. The egotism of a lifetime suddenly collapsed before the fascinations of Mary Berry. It was in vain that the old wit sought to conceal from himself and the world the nature of the feelings which had seized upon him. He made game of his vicissitude; he was in love—ah, yes!—but with both the charming sisters—with Agnes as well as Mary; they were his "twin wives," and might share his coronet between them if they liked. For a short space, indeed, he was almost entirely happy. Mary was gentle, intelligent, and appreciative; Agnes, gay and sprightly, made a perfect chaperon. They were his near neighbours at Twickenham, and night after night they would sit with him in his Strawberry Hill drawing-room, while, from his sofa, with an occasional pinch of snuff, he discoursed to them for endless magical hours, pouring out before them his whole treasury of anecdotes and reflections and quips and fancies and memories—old scandals, old frolics, old absurdities, old characters—the darling sixty years' accumulation of the most rapacious gossip who ever lived.

It was during these happy days—the springtime of his passion—that he wrote down for the sisters his *Reminiscences*, which have now been republished, from the original manuscripts, by the Clarendon Press.[1] The volume, elegantly printed, with elucidations by Mr. Paget Toynbee, two portraits, and some interesting "Notes of conversations with Lady Suffolk," now produced for the first time, is as delightful in its form as in its matter—delightful to handle, to look at, to browse over for an evening by the fire. In its polished, delicate pages the English eighteenth century is reflected for us, as in a diminishing mirror—St. James's, Sir Robert, a King or two, Mrs. Howard, old Sarah, Queen Caroline—miraculously small and neat; while Dance's admirable drawing shows us the author, almost, one might imagine, in the

[1] "Reminiscences, written by Mr. Horace Walpole in 1788, for the amusement of Miss Mary and Miss Agnes Berry." With Notes and Index by Paget Toynbee. (Oxford: Clarendon Press.)

act of composition, with his face so full of subtlety, experience, reticence, and sly urbanity.

But the happy days were not to last. Love grows cruel as he grows old; the arrow festers in the flesh; and a pleasant pang becomes a torture. Walpole could not be blinded for ever to the essential impossibility of his situation, and at last he was obliged to plumb his feelings to their depths. A dreadful blow fell when the sisters, accompanied by their father, left England on the grand tour. Their decision to do so had stunned him; their departure plunged him in grief; he was very old, and they were to be away for more than a year; would he ever see Mary again? Yet he bore up bravely, and his inimitable letters flowed over Europe in an unceasing stream. The crisis came when, on their return journey, the Berrys arranged to go back through France. It was in 1791, and the country was seething with the ferment of the Revolution. Walpole was terrified, and implored Mary to return by Germany; in vain. Then the old man's self-control utterly gave way. Fear, mortification, anger, and solicitude mastered him by turns; his agitation was boundless; he could talk of nothing but the Berrys, rush-

ing from person to person, pouring out, everywhere, to anybody, the palpitating tale of his
terrors and his griefs. London shrugged its shoulders: Lord Orford was ridiculous. The grim ghost
of Madame du Deffand must have smiled sar-
donically at the sight.

It was not merely the incompatibility of age
that made his case desperate; there was another
more fatal circumstance. Mary Berry herself was
passionately in love—with General O'Hara. He
was a middle-aged soldier of an old-fashioned
type, abounding in Irish energy, with a red and
black face and shining teeth; and when, in 1795, he
was made Governor of Gibraltar, she became engaged to marry him. The marriage itself was post-
poned, at her wish. She might have left Walpole
in his misery; and even her father, who was help-
less without her; but she could not leave her sister,
who was in the middle of a difficult love-affair,
and was every moment in need of her advice. "I
think I am doing right," she told O'Hara. "I am
sure I am consulting the peace and happiness of
those about me, and not my own." The General
sailed, and she never saw him again. At first their
correspondence was all that was most fitting. The

General poured out his gallantries, and Mary indulged in delightful visions of domesticity. She sketched in detail the balance-sheet of their future "establishment." Reducing their expenditure to a minimum, she came to the conclusion that £2,263 a year would be enough for them both. Of this sum, £58 would cover "the wages of four women servants—a housekeeper, a cook under her, a housemaid, and lady's maid"; while "liveries for the three men servants and the coachman" would cost £80 a year, and wine £100. But Mary's castle was all too truly in Spain. Before the year was out, it had vanished into thin air. She discovered that the "Old Cock of the Rock," as his military comrades called him, was keeping a couple of mistresses; expostulations followed, mutual anger, and finally a complete severance. She believed to the end of her life that if they could have met for twenty-four hours every difficulty would have disappeared; but it was not to be. The French War prevented O'Hara from returning to England, and in 1802 he died at his post.

Mary Berry was to live for half a century more, but she never recovered from this disaster. There, for the rest of her life, at the very basis of her existence, lay the iron fact of an irremediable dis-appointment. Thus her fate was the very reverse of Madame du Deffand's; the emotional tragedy, coming at the beginning of a long life instead of at the end, gave a sombre colour to the whole; and yet, in the structure of their minds, the two were curiously similar. Both were remarkable for reason and good sense, for a certain intellectual probity, for a disillusioned view of things, and for great strength of will. Between these two stern women, the figure of Horace Walpole makes a strange appearance—a creature all vanity, ele-gance, insinuation, and finesse—by far the most feminine of the three.

He died, leaving the sisters a house at Little Strawberry Hill and the interest on £4,000 for each of them for their lives. By a cruel irony of circumstance, her sister's love-affair, which had led Mary, so fatally, to postpone her marriage, turned out no less unfortunately than her own. Agnes had become engaged to a wealthy young cousin; but, at the last moment, the match had been broken off. The sisters never separated for the whole of their long lives. Agnes was cheerful, but a little vague in the head; she painted. Old

Mr. Berry was cheerful, but quite incompetent; he did nothing at all. Mary was intelligent, with enough character for three at the very least; and she did everything that had to be done, with consummate ease. Friends surrounded her. Walpole had launched the family into the highest society, where they had at once become very popular. His cousin, Mrs. Damer, was Mary's intimate and confidante. The Berry sisters—Blackberry and Gooseberry they were nicknamed by the malicious—were seen at every social function, and gradually became a social centre themselves. Among her other gifts Mary possessed a marvellous capacity for the part of hostess. Wherever she went—and she was constantly on the move—in North Audley Street, in Bath, in Paris, in Italy—it always happened that the most fashionable and the cleverest people grouped themselves about her. One winter, in Genoa, she seemed to create a civilization out of nothing; the little community gave a gasp of horror when she went away. Apparently there was nothing that she could not bring about in her drawing-room: she could even make Frenchmen hold their tongues; she could even make Englishmen talk.

But these were not her only accomplishments. Her masculine mind exercised itself over higher things. She read eagerly and long; she edited Walpole's papers; she studied political economy, appreciating Malthus and Free Trade. In Madame de Staël's opinion she was *"by far* the cleverest woman in England." She had literary ambitions, and brought out a book on "Social Life in England and France"; but her style failed to express the force of her mentality, so that her careful sentences are today unreadable. Had she been a man, she would not have shone as a writer, but as a political thinker or an administrator; and a man she should have been; with her massive, practical intelligence, she was born too early to be a successful woman. She felt this bitterly. Conscious of high powers, she declaimed against the miserable estate of women, which prevented her from using them. She might have been a towering leader, in thought or action; as it was, she was insignificant. So she said—"insignificant!" —repeating the word over and over again. "And nobody," she added, "ever suffered insignificance more unwillingly than myself."

Yet it was a mitigated insignificance, after all.

In 1817 old Mr. Berry died, and for another thirty years all that was distinguished in England and in France passed through the sisters' room in Curzon Street. As time went on, Mary grew ever grander and more vigorous. With old age, something like happiness seemed to come to her— though it was a happiness without serenity. Agnes chirped blithely by her side. Mrs. Damer had vanished, but her place was taken by Lady Charlotte Lindsay, who remained a faithful follower till her death. We catch a glimpse of the three ladies in Paris in 1834, when they were all in the neighbourhood of seventy. "The Berrys," Lady Granville tells us, "run up and down." Mary was the leader, prepotent, scolding, loud-voiced, and dressed in a pink sash. Agnes and Lady Charlotte fluttered along behind her. There was some laughter, but there was more admiration: Miss Berry was impossible to resist. Every one flocked to her evenings, as usual, and even critical Lady Granville was at her feet. She was friendly and true, said the Ambassadress, in spite of her frowns and hootings, and her departure would be regretted very much.

The *salon* in Curzon Street lasted on into the

Victorian age, and Thackeray would talk for
hours with the friend of Horace Walpole. The
lady was indeed a fascinating relic of an abolished
world, as she sat, large and formidable, bolt up-
right, in her black wig, with her rouged cheeks,
her commanding features, and her loud conversation, garnished with vigorous oaths. When, in
1852, both sisters died, aged eighty-nine and
eighty-eight, the eighteenth century finally vanished from the earth. So much was plain to the
habitués of Curzon Street; but they had failed to
realize the inner nature, the tragic under-tones,
of that spirit which had delighted them so won-
derfully with its energy and power. It was only
when Mary Berry's papers came to be examined
that the traces of her secret history appeared.
Among them was a description of a dream,
dreamt when she was nearly eighty, in which she
had found herself walking with Mrs. Damer by
a Southern shore, young again, and married to
General O'Hara. She was perfectly happy—so
happy that she prayed to die "before this beautiful vision of life fades, as fade it must from my
senses." Yet no!—she was about to have a child;
she must live to give him a child, she told Mrs.

Damer, and then she might die, "convinced that I have exhausted everything that can make life desirable. . . . Here I awoke with my eyes suffused with tears, to find myself a poor, feeble old soul, never having possessed either husband or child, and having long survived that friend whom my waking as well as my sleeping thoughts always recall to me, as the comfort and support of nearly thirty years of my sadly insignificant existence."

Madame de Lieven

ARISTOCRATS (no doubt) still exist; but they are shorn beings, for whom the wind is not tempered—powerless, out of place, and slightly ridiculous. For about a hundred years it has been so. The stages in the history of nobility may be reckoned by the different barricades it has put up to keep off the common multitude. The feudal lord used armour to separate him from the rest of the world; then, as civilization grew, it was found that a wig did almost as well; and there was a curious transition period (*temp.* Marlborough) when armour and wigs were worn at the same time. After that, armour vanished, and wigs were left, to rule splendidly through the eighteenth century, until the French Revolution. A fearful moment! Wigs went. Nevertheless the citadel still held out, for another barrier remained—the barrier of manners; and for a generation it was just possible to be an aristocrat on manners alone. Then, at last, about 1830, manners themselves

crumbled, undermined by the insidious perme-
ation of a new—a middle-class—behaviour; and
all was over. Madame de Lieven was one of the
supreme examples of the final period. Her manners were of the genuinely terrific kind. Surrounded by them, isolated as with an aseptic
spray, she swept on triumphantly, to survive un-
touched—so it seemed—amid an atmosphere alive
with the microbes of bourgeois disintegration. So
it seemed—for in fact something strange eventually happened. In her case, aristocracy, like some
viscous fluid flowing along, when it came to the
precipice did not plunge over the edge, but—such
was its strength, its inherent force of concentration—moved, as it had always moved, straight
onward, until it stuck out, an amazing semi-solid
projection, over the abyss. Only at long last was
there a melting; the laws of nature asserted themselves; and the inevitable, the deplorable, col-
lapse ensued.

Born in 1785, a Russian and a Benckendorf,
Madame de Lieven was by blood more than half
German, for her mother had come from Württem-
berg and her father's family was of Prussian origin.
From the first moment of her existence she was in

the highest sphere. Her mother had been the favourite companion of the Empress Marie, wife of
Paul I, and on her death the Empress had adopted
the young Benckendorfs and brought them up
under her own care. At the age of fifteen, Dorothea was taken from a convent and married to
the young Count de Lieven (or, more correctly,
Count Lieven without the "particule"; but it
would be pedantry to insist upon an accuracy
unknown to contemporaries) whose family was
no less closely connected with the Imperial house.
His mother had been the governess of the Emperor Paul's children; when her task was over,
she had retained the highest favour; and her son,
at the age of twenty-eight, was aide-de-camp to
the Emperor and Secretary for War. Paul I was
was murdered; but under the new Czar the family fortunes continued to prosper—the only change
being the transference of the Count de Lieven
from the army to the diplomatic service. In 1809
he was appointed Russian ambassador at Berlin;
and in 1812 he was moved to London, where he
and his wife were to remain for the next twenty-
two years.

The great world in those days was small—par-

ticularly the English one, which had been kept
in a vacuum for years by the Napoleonic War.
In 1812 a foreign embassy was a surprising
novelty in London, and the arrival of the Lievens
produced an excitement which turned to rapture
when it was discovered that the ambassadress was
endowed with social talents of the highest order.
She immediately became the fashion—and remained so for the rest of her life. That she possessed neither beauty nor intellect was probably
a positive advantage; she was attractive and
clever—that was enough. Her long gawky figure
and her too pronounced features were somehow
fascinating, and her accomplishments were exactly suited to her *milieu;* while she hated reading,
never opening a book except Madame de Sévigné's letters, she could be very entertaining in
four languages, and, if asked, could play on the
pianoforte extremely well. Whenever she appeared, life was enhanced and intensified. She became the intimate friend of several great hostesses
—Lady Holland, Lady Cowper, Lady Granville;
she was successfully adored by several men of
fashion—Lord Willoughby, Lord Gower, and (for
a short time—so it was whispered) the Prince

Regent himself. She was made a patroness of Almack's—the only foreign lady to receive the distinction. Exclusive, vigorous, tart, she went on her way rejoicing—and then there was a fresh development. The war over, the era of conferences opened. In 1818, at Aix-la-Chapelle, where all the ministers and diplomats of Europe were gathered together, she met Metternich, then at the beginning of his long career as the virtual ruler of Austria, and a new and serious love-affair immediately began. It lasted during the four years that elapsed between the Congress of Aix-la-Chapelle and that of Verona; and in Metternich's love-letters—extremely long and extremely metaphysical—the earlier stages of it may still be traced. The affair ended as suddenly as it had started. But this close relationship with the dominating figure in European politics had a profound effect on Madame de Lieven's life.

Henceforward, high diplomacy was to be her passion. She was nearly forty; it was time to be ambitious, to live by the head rather than the heart, to explore the mysteries of chanceries, to pull the strings of cabinets, to determine the fate of nations; she set to work with a will. Besides her native wits, she had two great assets—her position in English society, and the fact that her husband was a nonentity—she found that she could simply step into his place. Her first triumph came when the Czar Alexander entrusted her personally with an overture to Canning on the thorny question of Greece. Alexander's death and the accession of Nicholas was all to the good: her husband's mother received a princedom, and she herself in consequence became a Princess. At the same time Russia, abandoning the traditions of the Holy Alliance, drew nearer to England and the liberal policy of Canning. Madame de Lieven became the presiding genius of the new orientation; it was possibly owing to her influence with George IV that Canning obtained the Premiership; and it was certainly owing to her efforts that the Treaty of London was signed in 1827, by which the independence of Greece became an accomplished fact. After Canning's death, she formed a new connection—with Lord Grey. The great Whig Earl became one of the most ardent of her admirers. Sitting up in bed every morning, he made it his first task to compose an elaborate epistle to his Egeria, which, when it was completed, he carefully perfumed with musk. The precise nature of their relationship has never transpired. The tone of their correspondence seems to indicate a purely platonic attachment; but tones are deceitful, and Lord Grey was a man of many gallantries; however, he was sixty-eight. It is also doubtful who benefited most by the connection: possibly the lady's influence was less than she supposed. At any rate it is certain that when, on one occasion, she threatened a withdrawal of her favours unless the Prime Minister adopted a particular course, she was met with a regretful, an infinitely regretful, refusal; upon which she tactfully collapsed. But, on another occasion, it seems possible that her advice produced an important consequence. When Lord Grey took office, who was to be Foreign Minister? Lady Cowper was Madame de Lieven's great friend, and Palmerston was Lady Cowper's lover. At their request, Madame de Lieven pressed the claims of Palmerston upon the Premier, and Palmerston was appointed. If this was indeed the result of her solicitations, the triumphant Princess was to find before long that she had got more than she had bargained for.

In the meantime, all went swimmingly. There

was always some intriguing concoction on the
European table—a revolution in Portugal—the
affairs of Belgium to be settled—a sovereign to be
found for Greece—and Madame de Lieven's fin-
ger was invariably in the pie. So we see her, in the
Memoirs and Letters of the time, gliding along in
brilliant activity, a radiating focus of enjoyment,
except—ah! it was her one horror!—when she
found herself with a bore. If it was her highest
felicity to extract, in an excited *tête-à-tête*, the
latest piece of diplomatic gossip from a Cabinet
Minister, her deepest agony was to be forced to
mark time with undistinguished underlings, or—
worst of all!—some literary person. On such oc-
casions she could not conceal her despair—indeed
she hardly wished to—even from the most eminent—even from the great Châteaubriand himself. "Quand elle se trouve avec des gens de mé-
rite," he acidly noted, "sa stérilité se tait; elle
revêt sa nullité d'un air supérieur d'ennui, comme
si elle avait le droit d'être ennuyée." She only
admitted one exception: for royal personages very
great allowances might be made. A royal bore,
indeed, was almost a contradiction in terms; such
a flavour of mysterious suavity hovered for ever

round those enchanted beings. She was always at her best with them, and for her own particular royalties—for the Czar and the whole imperial family—no considerations, no exertions, no adulations could be too great. She corresponded personally with her imperial master upon every twist and turn of the international situation, and yet there were tedious wretches . . . she would not bear it, she would be ruthless, they should be *écrasés*—and she lifted her black eyebrows till they almost vanished and drew herself up to her thinnest height. She looked like some strange animal —what was it? Somebody said that Madame Appony, another slender, tall ambassadress, was like a giraffe, and that she and Madame de Lieven were of the same species. "Mais non!" said Madame Alfred de Noailles, "ce n'est pas la même classe: l'une mangera l'autre et n'aura qu'un mauvais repas"—"One sees Lieven," was Lady Granville's comment, "crunching the meek Appony's bones." Every one was a little afraid of her —every one, that is to say, except Lady Holland; for "Old Madagascar" knew no fear. One day, at a party, having upset her work-basket, she calmly turned to the ambassadress with, "Pick it up, my dear, pick it up!" And Madame de Lieven went down on her knees and obeyed. "Such a sight was never seen before," said Lady Granville.

Lady Holland—yes; but there was also somebody else; there was Palmerston. Madame de Lieven, having (so she was convinced) got him his appointment as Foreign Secretary, believed that she could manage him; he was, she declared, "un très-petit esprit"; the mistake was gross, and it was fatal. In 1834, Palmerston appointed Stratford Canning ambassador to Russia; but the Emperor disliked him, and let it be known, through Madame de Lieven, that he was unwilling to receive him. Palmerston, however, persisted in his choice, in spite of all the arguments of the ambassadress, who lost her temper, appealed to Lord Grey—in vain, and then—also in vain—tried to get up an agitation in the Cabinet. Finally she advised the Czar to stand firm, for Palmerston, she said, would give way when it came to the point. Accordingly, it was officially stated that Stratford Canning would not be received in Russia. The result, however, was far from Madame de Lieven's expectations. Palmerston had had enough of female interferences, and he decided to take this opportunity of putting an end to them altogether. He appointed no ambassador, and for months the English business in St. Petersburg was transacted by a *chargé d'affaires*. Then there happened precisely what the wily minister had foreseen. The Emperor could support the indignity no longer; he determined to retort in kind; and he recalled the Lievens.

So ended the official life of the Princess. The blow was severe—the pain of parting was terrible —but, as it turned out, this was only the beginning of misfortune. In the following year, her two youngest sons died of scarlet fever; her own health was broken; stricken down by grief and illness, she gave up the Court appointment with which her services had been rewarded, and went to live in Paris. Suddenly she received a peremptory order of recall. Nicholas, with autocratic caprice, had flown into a fury; the Princess must return! Her husband, seeing that a chance of self-assertion had at last come to him, fell in with the Emperor's wishes. A third son died; and the Prince was forbidden to communicate the fact to his wife; she only learnt it, months later, when one of her letters to her son was returned to her, with the word "mort" on the envelope. After that, there was a hectic correspondence, the Prince at one moment actually threatening to cut off his wife's supplies if she remained in Paris. She would not budge, however, and eventually the storm blew over; but the whole system of Madame de Lieven's existence had received a terrible shock. "Quel pays!" she exclaimed in her anguish. "Quel maître! Quel père!"

The instinct which had kept her in Paris was a sound one; for there, in that friendly soil, she was able to strike fresh roots and to create for herself an establishment that was almost a home. Her irrepressible social activities once more triumphed. Installed in Talleyrand's old house at the corner of the Rue de Rivoli and the Rue St. Florentin, with an outlook over the Place de la Concorde, she held her nightly *salon*, and, for another twenty years, revived the glories of her London reign. Though no longer in any official situation, she was still perpetually occupied with the highest politics, was still the terror of embassies, still the delight of the worldly and the great. Still, in her pitiless exclusiveness, she would *écraser* from time to time some wretched creature from another sphere. "Monsieur, je ne vous connais pas," she said in icy tones to a gentleman who presented himself one evening in her *salon*. He reminded her of how often they had met at Ems, in the summer —had taken the waters together—surely she must remember him. "Non, Monsieur," was the adamantine reply, and the poor man slunk away, having learnt the lesson that friendship at Ems and friendship in Paris are two very different things.

Such was the appearance; but in fact something strange had happened: Madame de Lieven's aristocracy was trembling over the abyss. The crash came on June 24, 1837—the date is significant: it was four days after the accession of Queen Victoria—when, worn out by domestic grief, disillusioned, embittered, unable to resist any longer the permeations of the Time Spirit, the Princess fell into the arms of Monsieur Guizot. Fate had achieved an almost exaggerated irony. For Guizot was the living epitome of all that was most middle-class. Infinitely respectable, a Protestant, the father of a family, having buried two wives, a learned historian, he had just given up the portfolio of public instruction, and was clearly destined to be the leading spirit of the bourgeois monarchy of Louis-Philippe. He was fifty years old. His first wife had been a child of the *ancien régime*, but he had tamed her, turned her thoughts towards duty and domesticity, induced her to write improving stories for the young, until at last, suddenly feeling that she could bear it no longer, she had taken refuge in death while he was reading aloud to her a sermon by Bossuet on the immortality of the soul. His second wife—the niece of the first—had needed no such pressure; naturally all that could be wished, she wrote several volumes of improving stories for the young quite of her own accord, while reflections upon the beneficence of the Creator flowed from her at the slightest provocation; but she too had died; his eldest son had died; and the bereaved Guizot was left alone with his high-mindedness. Madame de Lieven was fifty-two. It seemed an incredible love-affair—so much so that Charles Greville, who had known her intimately all his life, refused to believe that it was anything but a "social and political" *liaison*. But the wits of Paris thought otherwise. It was noticed that Guizot was always to be found in the house in the Rue St. Florentin.

The malicious Mérimée told the story of how, after a party at the Princess's, he had been the last to leave—except Guizot; how, having forgotten something, he had returned to the drawing-room, and found that the Minister had already taken off the ribbon (the "grand cordon") of the Legion of Honour. A chuckle—a chuckle from beyond the tomb—reached the world from Châteaubriand. "Le ridicule attendait à Paris Madame de Lieven. Un doctrinaire grave est tombé aux pieds d'Omphale: 'Amour, tu perdis Troie.' " And the wits of Paris were right. The *liaison*, certainly, was strengthened by political and social interests, but its basis was sentimental passion. The testimony of a long series of letters puts that beyond a doubt. In this peculiar correspondence, pedantry, adoration, platitudes, and suburban *minauderies* form a compound for which one hardly knows whether smiles or tears are the appropriate reaction. When Guizot begins a love-letter with—"Le Cardinal de Retz dit quelque part," one can only be delighted, but when Madame de Lieven exclaims, "Ah! que j'aurais besoin d'être gouvernée! Pourquoi ne me gouvernez-vous pas?" one is positively embarrassed. One feels that one is committing an unpardonable—a deliciously unpardonable—indiscretion, as one overhears the cooings of these antiquated doves. "Si vous pouviez voir," he says, with exquisite originality, "tout ce qu'il y a dans mon cœur, si profond, si fort, si éternel, si tendre, si triste." And she answers, "Maintenant, je voudrais la tranquillité, la paix du cottage, votre amour, le mien, rien que cela. Ah! mon ami, c'est là le vrai bonheur." La paix du cottage! Can this be really and truly Madame de Lieven?

Yet there was a point at which she did draw the line. After the death of the Prince in 1839, it was inevitable that there should be a suggestion of marriage. But it faded away. They were never united by any other vows than those which they had sworn to each other in the sight of heaven. It was rumoured that the difficulty was simply one of nomenclature. Guizot (one would expect it) judged that he would be humiliated if his wife's name were not his own; and the Princess, though wishing to be governed, recoiled at that. "Ma chère, on dit que vous allez épouser Guizot," said a friend. "Est-ce vrai?" "Oh! ma chère," was the reply, "me voyez-vous annoncée Madame Guizot!" Was this the last resistance of the aristocrat? Or was it perhaps, in reality, the final proof that Madame de Lieven was an aristocrat no longer?

The idyll only ended with death—though there were a few interruptions. In 1848, revolution forced the lovers to fly to England; it also precipitated the aged Metternich, with a new young wife, upon these hospitable shores. The quartet spent a fortnight together at Brighton; until their discreet conversations were ended for ever by the restoration of order; and the *salon* in the Rue St. Florentin was opened again. But a new dispensation was beginning, in which there was no place for the old minister of Louis-Philippe. Guizot stood aside; and, though Madame de Lieven continued to wield an influence under the Second Empire, it was a gradually declining one. The Crimean War came as a shattering blow. She had made it up with the Czar; their correspondence was once more in full swing; this was known, and, when war came, she was forced to leave Paris for Brussels. Her misery was complete, but it only lasted for eighteen months. She crept back on the plea of health, and Napoleon, leniently winking at her presence, allowed her to remain—allowed her at last to re-open, very gingerly, her *salon*. But everything now was disappearing, disintegrating, shimmering away. She was in her seventy-second year; she was ill and utterly exhausted; she was dying. Guizot, a veteran too, was perpetually at her bedside; she begged him at last to leave her—to go into the next room for a little. He obeyed, and she was dead when he returned to her. She had left a note for him, scribbled in pencil—"Je vous remercie des vingt années d'affection et de bonheur. Ne m'oubliez pas. Adieu, Adieu." At the last moment, with those simple and touching words, the old grandeur —the original essence that was Dorothea Benckendorf—had come into its own again.

SIX ENGLISH HISTORIANS

Hume

IN WHAT resides the most characteristic virtue of humanity? In good works? Possibly. In the creation of beautiful objects? Perhaps. But some would look in a different direction, and find it in detachment. To all such David Hume must be a great saint in the calendar; for no mortal being was ever more completely divested of the trammels of the personal and the particular, none ever practised with a more consummate success the divine art of impartiality. And certainly to have no axe to grind is something very noble and very rare. It may be said to be the antithesis of the bestial. A series of creatures might be constructed, arranged according to their diminishing interest in the immediate environment, which would begin with the amoeba and end with the mathematician. In pure mathematics the maximum of detachment appears to be reached: the mind moves in an infinitely complicated pattern, which is absolutely free from temporal considerations. Yet

this very freedom—the essential condition of the
mathematician's activity—perhaps gives him an
unfair advantage. He can only be wrong—he
cannot cheat. But the metaphysician can. The
problems with which he deals are of overwhelming importance to himself and the rest of humanity; and it is his business to treat them with
an exactitude as unbiassed as if they were some
puzzle in the theory of numbers. That is his business—and his glory. In the mind of a Hume one
can watch at one's ease this superhuman balance
of contrasting opposites—the questions of so profound a moment, the answers of so supreme a
calm. And the same beautiful quality may be
traced in the current of his life, in which the wisdom of philosophy so triumphantly interpene-
trated the vicissitudes of the mortal lot.

His history falls into three stages—youth, maturity, repose. The first was the most important.
Had Hume died at the age of twenty-six his real
work in the world would have been done, and
his fame irrevocably established. Born in 1711,
the younger son of a small Scottish landowner, he
was very early dominated by that passion for literary pursuits which never left him for the rest of

his life. When he was twenty-two one of those crises occurred—both physical and mental—which not uncommonly attack young men of genius when their adolescence is over, and determine the lines of their destiny. Hume was suddenly overcome by restlessness, ill-health, anxiety and hesitation. He left home, went to London, and then to Bristol, where, with the idea of making an independent fortune, he became a clerk in a merchant's office. "But," as he wrote long afterwards in his autobiography, "in a few months I found that scene totally unsuitable to me." No wonder; and then it was that, by a bold stroke of instinctive wisdom, he took the strange step which was the starting-point of his career. He went to France, where he remained for three years—first at Rheims, then at La Flèche, in Anjou—entirely alone, with only just money enough to support an extremely frugal existence, and with only the vaguest prospects before him. During those years he composed his *Treatise of Human Nature*, the masterpiece which contains all that is most important in his thought. The book opened a new era in philosophy. The last vestiges of theological prepossessions—which were still faintly visible in

Descartes and Locke—were discarded; and reason, in all her strength and all her purity, came into her own. It is in the sense that Hume gives one of being committed absolutely to reason—of following wherever reason leads, with a complete, and even reckless, confidence—that the great charm of his writing consists. But it is not only that: one is not alone; one is in the company of a supremely competent guide. With astonishing vigour, with heavenly lucidity, Hume leads one through the confusion and the darkness of speculation. One has got into an aeroplane, which has glided imperceptibly from the ground; with thrilling ease one mounts and mounts; and, supported by the mighty power of intellect, one looks out, to see the world below one, as one has never seen it before. In the Treatise there is something that does not appear again in Hume's work—a feeling of excitement—the excitement of discovery. At moments he even hesitates, and stands back, amazed at his own temerity. "The *intense* view of these manifold contradictions and imperfections in human reason has so wrought upon me, and heated my brain, that I am ready to reject all belief and reasoning, and can look upon no opinion even as more probable or likely than another. Where am I, or what? From what causes do I derive my existence, and to what condition shall I return? Whose favour shall I court, and whose anger must I dread? What beings surround me? and on whom have I any influence, or who have influence on me? I am confounded with all these questions, and begin to fancy myself in the most deplorable condition imaginable, environed with the deepest darkness, and utterly deprived of the use of every member and faculty." And then his courage returns once more, and he speeds along on his exploration.

The Treatise, published in 1738, was a complete failure. For many years more Hume remained in poverty and insignificance. He eked out a living by precarious secretaryships, writing meanwhile a series of essays on philosophical, political and aesthetic subjects, which appeared from time to time in small volumes, and gradually brought him a certain reputation. It was not till he was over forty, when he was made librarian to the Faculty of Advocates in Edinburgh, that his position became secure. The appointment gave him not only a small competence, but the command of a large library; and he determined to write the history of England—a task which occupied him for the next ten years.

The History was a great success; many editions were printed; and in his own day it was chiefly as a historian that Hume was known to the general public. After his death his work continued for many years the standard history of England, until, with a new age, new fields of knowledge were opened up and a new style of historical writing became fashionable. The book is highly typical of the eighteenth century. It was an attempt—one of the very earliest—to apply intelligence to the events of the past. Hitherto, with very few exceptions (Bacon's *Henry the Seventh* was one of them) history had been in the hands of memoir writers like Commines and Clarendon, or moralists like Bossuet. Montesquieu, in his *Considérations sur les Romains*, had been the first to break the new ground; but his book, brilliant and weighty as it was, must be classed rather as a philosophical survey than a historical narration. Voltaire, almost exactly contemporary with Hume, was indeed a master of narrative, but was usually too much occupied with discrediting Christianity to be a satisfactory historian. Hume had no such *arrière pensée;* he only wished to tell the truth as he saw it, with clarity and elegance. And he succeeded. In his volumes—especially those on the Tudors and Stuarts—one may still find entertainment and even instruction. Hume was an extremely intelligent man, and anything that he had to say on English history could not fail to be worth attending to. But, unfortunately, mere intelligence is not itself quite enough to make a great historian. It was not simply that Hume's knowledge of his subject was insufficient—that an enormous number of facts, which have come into view since he wrote, have made so many of his statements untrue and so many of his comments unmeaning; all that is serious, but it is not more serious than the circumstance that his cast of mind was in reality ill-fitted for the task he had undertaken. The virtues of a metaphysician are the vices of a historian. A generalised, colourless, unimaginative view of things is admirable when one is considering the law of causality, but one needs something else if one has to describe Queen Elizabeth.

This fundamental weakness is materialised in the style of the History. Nothing could be more enchanting than Hume's style when he is discussing philosophical subjects. The grace and clarity of exquisite writing are enhanced by a touch of colloquialism—the tone of a polished conversation. A personality—a most engaging personality—just appears. The cat-like touches of ironic malice—hints of something very sharp behind the velvet—add to the effect. "Nothing," Hume concludes, after demolishing every argument in favour of the immortality of the soul, "could set in a fuller light the infinite obligations which mankind have to divine revelation, since we find that no other medium could ascertain this great and important truth." The sentence is characteristic of Hume's writing at its best, where the pungency of the sense varies in direct proportion with the mildness of the expression. But such effects are banished from the History. A certain formality, which Hume doubtless supposed was required by the dignity of the subject, is interposed between the reader and the author; an almost completely latinised vocabulary makes vividness impossible; and a habit of *oratio obliqua* has a deadening effect. We shall never know exactly what Henry the Second said—in some uncouth dialect of French or English—in his final exasperation against Thomas of Canterbury; but it was certainly something about "a set of fools and cowards," and "vengeance," and "an upstart clerk." Hume, however, preferred to describe the scene as follows: "The King himself being vehemently agitated, burst forth with an exclamation against his servants, whose want of zeal, he said, had so long left him exposed to the enterprises of that ungrateful and imperious prelate." Such phrasing, in conjunction with the Middle Ages, is comic. The more modern centuries seem to provide a more appropriate field for urbanity, aloofness and common sense. The measured cynicism of Hume's comments on Cromwell, for instance, still makes good reading—particularly as a corrective to the *O, altitudo!* sentimentalities of Carlyle.

Soon after his completion of the History Hume went to Paris as the secretary to the English Ambassador. He was now a celebrity, and French society fell upon him with delirious delight. He was flattered by princes, worshipped by fine ladies, and treated as an oracle by the *philosophes*. To such an extent did he become the fashion that it

was at last positively *de rigueur* to have met him,
and a lady who, it was discovered, had not even
seen the great philosopher, was banished from
Court. His appearance, so strangely out of keeping with mental agility, added to the fascination.
"His face," wrote one of his friends, "was broad
and flat, his mouth wide, and without any other
expression than that of imbecility. His eyes vacant
and spiritless, and the corpulence of his whole
person was far better fitted to communicate the
idea of a turtle-eating alderman than of a refined
philosopher." All this was indeed delightful to the
French. They loved to watch the awkward affa-
bility of the uncouth figure, to listen in rapt attention to the extraordinary French accent, and
when, one evening, at a party, the adorable man
appeared in a charade as a sultan between two
lovely ladies and could only say, as he struck his
chest, over and over again, "Eh bien, mesde-
moiselles, eh bien, vous voilà donc!" their ecstasy
reached its height. It seemed indeed almost impossible to believe in this combination of the
outer and inner man. Even his own mother never
got below the surface. "Our Davie," she is re-
ported to have said, "is a fine good-natured

cratur, but uncommon wake-minded." In no sense whatever was this true. Hume was not only brilliant as an abstract thinker and a writer; he was no less competent in the practical affairs of life. In the absence of the Ambassador he was left in Paris for some months as *chargé d'affaires*, and his dispatches still exist to show that he understood diplomacy as well as ratiocination.

Entirely unmoved by the raptures of Paris, Hume returned to Edinburgh, at last a prosperous and wealthy man. For seven years he lived in his native capital, growing comfortably old amid leisure, books, and devoted friends. It is to this final period of his life that those pleasant legends belong which reveal the genial charm, the happy temperament, of the philosopher. There is the story of the tallow-chandler's wife, who arrived to deliver a monitory message from on High, but was diverted from her purpose by a tactful order for an enormous number of candles. There is the well-known tale of the weighty philosopher getting stuck in the boggy ground at the base of the Castle rock, and calling on a passing old woman to help him out. She doubted whether any help should be given to the author of the Essay on

Miracles. "But, my good woman, does not your religion as a Christian teach you to do good, even to your enemies?" "That may be," was the reply, "but ye shallna get out of that till ye become a Christian yersell: and repeat the Lord's Prayer and the Belief"—a feat that was accomplished with astonishing alacrity. And there is the vision of the mountainous metaphysician seated, amid a laughing party of young ladies, on a chair that was too weak for him, and suddenly subsiding to the ground.

In 1776, when Hume was sixty-five, an internal complaint, to which he had long been subject, completely undermined his health, and recovery became impossible. For many months he knew he was dying, but his mode of life remained unaltered, and, while he gradually grew weaker, his cheerfulness continued unabated. With ease, with gaiety, with the simplicity of perfect taste, he gently welcomed the inevitable. This wonderful equanimity lasted till the very end. There was no ostentation of stoicism, much less any Addisonian dotting of death-bed i's. Not long before he died he amused himself by writing his autobiography —a model of pointed brevity. In one of his last conversations—it was with Adam Smith—he composed an imaginary conversation between himself and Charon, after the manner of Lucian: " 'Have a little patience, good Charon, I have been endeavouring to open the eyes of the Public. If I live a few years longer, I may have the satisfaction of seeing the downfall of some of the prevailing systems of superstition.' But Charon would then lose all temper and decency. 'You loitering rogue, that will not happen these many hundred years. Do you fancy I will grant you a lease for so long a term? Get into the boat this instant, you lazy, loitering rogue.' " Within a few days of his death he wrote a brief letter to his old friend, the Comtesse de Boufflers; it was the final expression of a supreme detachment. "My disorder," he said, "is a diarrhoea, or disorder in my bowels, which has been gradually undermining me these two years; but, within these six months, has been visibly hastening me to my end. I see death approach gradually, without anxiety or regret. I salute you, with great affection and regard, for the last time."

Gibbon

HAPPINESS is the word that immediately rises to the mind at the thought of Edward Gibbon: and happiness in its widest connotation —including good fortune as well as enjoyment. Good fortune, indeed, followed him from the cradle to the grave in the most tactful way possible; occasionally it appeared to fail him; but its absence always turned out to be a blessing in disguise. Out of a family of seven he alone had the luck to survive—but only with difficulty; and the maladies of his childhood opened his mind to the pleasures of study and literature. His mother died; but her place was taken by a devoted aunt, whose care brought him through the dangerous years of adolescence to a vigorous manhood. His misadventures at Oxford saved him from becoming a don. His exile to Lausanne, by giving him a command of the French language, initiated him into European culture, and at the same time enabled him to lay the foundations of his scholarship. His

father married again; but his stepmother remained childless and became one of his dearest
friends. He fell in love; the match was forbidden;
and he escaped the dubious joys of domestic life
with the future Madame Necker. While he was
allowed to travel on the Continent, it seemed
doubtful for some time whether his father would
have the resources or the generosity to send him
over the Alps into Italy. His fate hung in the balance; but at last his father produced the necessary five hundred pounds and, in the autumn of
1764, Rome saw her historian. His father died at
exactly the right moment, and left him exactly
the right amount of money. At the age of thirty-
three Gibbon found himself his own master, with
a fortune just sufficient to support him as an English gentleman of leisure and fashion. For ten
years he lived in London, a member of Parliament, a placeman, and a diner-out, and during
those ten years he produced the first three volumes of his History. After that he lost his place,
failed to obtain another, and, finding his income
unequal to his expenses, returned to Lausanne,
where he took up his residence in the house of a
friend, overlooking the Lake of Geneva. It was

the final step in his career, and no less fortunate than all the others. In Lausanne he was rich once more, he was famous, he enjoyed a delightful combination of retirement and society. Before another ten years were out he had completed his History; and in ease, dignity, and absolute satisfaction his work in this world was accomplished.

One sees in such a life an epitome of the blessings of the eighteenth century—the wonderful μηδὲν ἄγαν of that most balmy time—the rich fruit ripening slowly on the sun-warmed wall, and coming inevitably to its delicious perfection. It is difficult to imagine, at any other period in history, such a combination of varied qualities, so beautifully balanced—the profound scholar who was also a brilliant man of the world—the votary of cosmopolitan culture, who never for a moment ceased to be a supremely English "character." The ten years of Gibbon's life in London afford an astonishing spectacle of interacting energies. By what strange power did he succeed in producing a masterpiece of enormous erudition and perfect form, while he was leading the gay life of a man about town, spending his evenings at White's or Boodle's or the Club, attending Parliament, oscillating between his house in Bentinck Street, his country cottage at Hampton Court, and his little establishment at Brighton, spending his summers in Bath or Paris, and even, at odd moments, doing a little work at the Board of Trade, to show that his place was not entirely a sinecure? Such a triumph could only have been achieved by the sweet reasonableness of the eighteenth century. "Monsieur Gibbon n'est point mon homme," said Rousseau. Decidedly! The prophet of the coming age of sentiment and romance could have nothing in common with such a nature. It was not that the historian was a mere frigid observer of the golden mean—far from it. He was full of fire and feeling. His youth had been at moments riotous—night after night he had reeled hallooing down St. James's Street. Old age did not diminish the natural warmth of his affections; the beautiful letter—a model of its kind—written on the death of his aunt, in his fiftieth year, is a proof of it. But the fire and the feeling were controlled and co-ordinated. Boswell was a Rousseau-ite, one of the first of the Romantics, an inveterate sentimentalist, and nothing could be more complete than the contrast between his career and Gibbon's.

He, too, achieved a glorious triumph; but it was by dint of the sheer force of native genius asserting itself over the extravagance and disorder of an agitated life—a life which, after a desperate struggle, seemed to end at last in darkness and shipwreck. With Gibbon there was never any struggle: everything came naturally to him—learning and dissipation, industry and indolence, affection and scepticism—in the correct proportions; and he enjoyed himself up to the very end.

To complete the picture one must notice another antithesis: the wit, the genius, the massive intellect, were housed in a physical mould that was ridiculous. A little figure, extraordinarily rotund, met the eye, surmounted by a top-heavy head, with a button nose, planted amid a vast expanse of cheek and ear, and chin upon chin rolling downward. Nor was this appearance only; the odd shape reflected something in the inner man. Mr. Gibbon, it was noticed, was always slightly over-dressed; his favourite wear was flowered velvet. He was a little vain, a little pompous; at the first moment one almost laughed; then one forgot everything under the fascination of that even flow of admirably intelligent, exquisitely turned, and most amusing sentences. Among all his other merits this obviously ludicrous egotism took its place. The astonishing creature was able to make a virtue even of absurdity. Without that touch of nature he would have run the risk of being too much of a good thing; as it was there was no such danger; he was preposterous and a human being.

It is not difficult to envisage the character and the figure; what seems strange, and remote, and hard to grasp is the connection between this individual and the decline and fall of the Roman Empire. The paradox, indeed, is so complete as to be almost romantic. At a given moment—October 15, 1764—at a given place—the Capitoline Hill, outside the church of Aracoeli—the impact occurred between the serried centuries of Rome and Edward Gibbon. His life, his work, his fame, his place in the history of civilisation, followed from that circumstance. The point of his achievement lay precisely in the extreme improbability of it. The utter incongruity of those combining elements produced the masterpiece—the gigantic ruin of Europe through a thousand years, mirrored in the mind of an eighteenth-century English gentleman.

How was the miracle accomplished? Needless to say, Gibbon was a great artist—one of those rare spirits, with whom a vital and penetrating imagination and a supreme capacity for general conceptions express themselves instinctively in an appropriate form. That the question has ever been not only asked but seriously debated, whether History was an art, is certainly one of the curiosities of human ineptitude. What else can it possibly be? It is obvious that History is not a science: it is obvious that History is not the accumulation of facts, but the relation of them. Only the pedantry of incomplete academic persons could have given birth to such a monstrous supposition. Facts relating to the past, when they are collected without art, are compilations; and compilations, no doubt, may be useful; but they are no more History than butter, eggs, salt and herbs are an omelette. That Gibbon was a great artist, therefore, is implied in the statement that he was a great historian; but what is interesting is the particular nature of his artistry. His whole genius was pre-eminently classical; order, lucidity, balance, precision—the great classical qualities—dominate his work; and his History is chiefly re-

markable as one of the supreme monuments of
Classic Art in European literature.

"L'ordre est ce qu'il y a de plus rare dans les
opérations de l'esprit." Gibbon's work is a magnificent illustration of the splendid dictum of
Fénelon. He brought order out of the enormous
chaos of his subject—a truly stupendous achievement! With characteristic good fortune, indeed,
the material with which he had to cope was still
just not too voluminous to be digested by a single
extremely competent mind. In the following century even a Gibbon would have collapsed under
the accumulated mass of knowledge at his dis-
posal. As it was, by dint of a superb constructive
vision, a serene self-confidence, a very acute judgment, and an astonishing facility in the manipu-
lation of material, he was able to dominate the
known facts. To dominate, nothing more; anything else would have been foreign to his purpose.
He was a classicist; and his object was not comprehension but illumination. He drove a straight,
firm road through the vast unexplored forest of
Roman history; his readers could follow with easy
pleasure along the wonderful way; they might
glance, as far as their eyes could reach, into the

entangled recesses on either side of them; but they were not invited to stop, or wander, or camp out, or make friends with the natives; they must be content to look and to pass on.

It is clear that Gibbon's central problem was the one of exclusion: how much, and what, was he to leave out? This was largely a question of scale—always one of the major difficulties in literary composition—and it appears from several passages in the Autobiographies that Gibbon paid particular attention to it. Incidentally it may be observed that the six Autobiographies were not so much excursions in egotism—though no doubt it is true that Gibbon was not without a certain fondness for what he himself called "the most disgusting of the pronouns"—as exercises on the theme of scale. Every variety of compression and expansion is visible among those remarkable pages; but apparently, since the manuscripts were left in an unfinished state, Gibbon still felt, after the sixth attempt, that he had not discovered the right solution. Even with the scale of the History he was not altogether satisfied; the chapters on Christianity, he thought, might, with further labour, have been considerably reduced. But, even more fundamental than the element of scale, there was something else that, in reality, conditioned the whole treatment of his material, the whole scope and nature of his History; and that was the style in which it was written. The style once fixed, everything else followed. Gibbon was well aware of this. He wrote his first chapter three times over, his second and third twice; then at last he was satisfied, and after that he wrote on without a hitch. In particular the problem of exclusion was solved. Gibbon's style is probably the most exclusive in literature. By its very nature it bars out a great multitude of human energies. It makes sympathy impossible, it takes no cognisance of passion, it turns its back upon religion with a withering smile. But that was just what was wanted. Classic beauty came instead. By the penetrating influence of style—automatically, inevitably—lucidity, balance and precision were everywhere introduced; and the miracle of order was established over the chaos of a thousand years.

Of course the Romantics raised a protest. "Gibbon's style," said Coleridge, "is detestable; but," he added, "it is not the worst thing about him." Critics of the later nineteenth century were less consistent. They admired Gibbon for everything except his style, imagining that his History would have been much improved if it had been written in some other way; they did not see that, if it had been written in any other way, it would have ceased to exist; just as St. Paul's would cease to exist if it were rebuilt in Gothic. Obsessed by the colour and movement of romantic prose, they were blind to the subtlety, the clarity, the continuous strength of Gibbon's writing. Gibbon could turn a bold phrase with the best of them— "the fat slumbers of the Church," for instance— if he wanted to; but he very rarely wanted to; such effects would have disturbed the easy, close-knit, homogeneous surface of his work. His use of words is, in fact, extremely delicate. When, describing St. Simeon Stylites on his pillar, he speaks of "this last and lofty station," he succeeds, with the least possible emphasis, merely by the combination of those two alliterative epithets with that particular substantive, in making the whole affair ridiculous. One can almost see his shoulders shrug. The nineteenth century found him pompous; they did not relish the irony beneath the pomp. He produces some of his most delightful effects by rhythm alone. In the *Vindication*—a work which deserves to be better known, for it shows us Gibbon, as one sees him nowhere else, really letting himself go—there is an admirable example of this. "I still think," he says, in reply to a criticism by Dr. Randolph, "I still think that an hundred Bishops, with Athanasius at their head, were as competent judges of the discipline of the fourth century, as even the Lady Margaret's Professor of Divinity in the University of Oxford." Gibbon's irony, no doubt, is the salt of his work; but, like all irony, it is the product of style. It was not for nothing that he read through every year the *Lettres Provinciales* of Pascal. From this point of view it is interesting to compare him with Voltaire. The irony of the great Frenchman was a flashing sword—extreme, virulent, deadly —a terrific instrument of propaganda. Gibbon uses the weapon with far more delicacy; he carves his enemy "as a dish fit for the Gods"; his mocking is aloof, almost indifferent, and perhaps, in the long run, for that very reason, even more effective.

At every period of his life Gibbon is a pleasant

thing to contemplate, but perhaps most pleasant of all in the closing weeks of it, during his last visit to England. He had hurried home from Lausanne to join his friend Lord Sheffield, whose wife had died suddenly, and who, he felt, was in need of his company. The journey was no small proof of his affectionate nature; old age was approaching; he was corpulent, gouty and accustomed to every comfort; and the war of the French Revolution was raging in the districts through which he had to pass. But he did not hesitate, and after skirting the belligerent armies in his chaise, arrived safely in England. After visiting Lord Sheffield he proceeded to Bath, to stay with his stepmother. The amazing little figure, now almost spherical, bowled along the Bath Road in the highest state of exhilaration. "I am always," he told his friend, "so much delighted and improved with this union of ease and motion, that, were not the expense enormous, I would travel every year some hundred miles, more especially in England." Mrs. Gibbon, a very old lady, but still full of vitality, worshipped her stepson, and the two spent ten days together, talking, almost always têtc-à-tête, for ten hours a day. Then the historian went off to Althorpe, where he spent a happy morning with Lord Spencer, looking at early editions of Cicero. And so back to London. In London a little trouble arose. A protuberance in the lower part of his person, which, owing to years of characteristic *insouciance*, had grown to extraordinary proportions, required attention; an operation was necessary; but it went off well, and there seemed to be no danger. Once more Mr. Gibbon dined out. Once more he was seen, in his accustomed attitude, with advanced forefinger, addressing the company, and rapping his snuff box at the close of each particularly pointed phrase. But illness came on again—nothing very serious. The great man lay in bed discussing how much longer he would live—he was fifty-six—ten years, twelve years, or perhaps twenty. He ate some chicken and drank three glasses of madeira. Life seemed almost as charming as usual. Next morning, getting out of bed for a necessary moment, "Je suis plus adroit," he said with his odd smile to his French valet. Back in bed again, he muttered something more, a little incoherently, lay back among the pillows, dozed, half-woke, dozed again, and became unconscious—for ever.

Macaulay

IN APOLLO's house there are many mansions; there is even one (unexpectedly enough) for the Philistine. So complex and various are the elements of literature that no writer can be damned on a mere enumeration of faults. He may always possess merits which make up for everything; if he loses on the swings, he may win on the roundabouts. Macaulay—whatever the refined and the sublime may say to the contrary—is an example of this. A coarse texture of mind—a metallic style—an itch for the obvious and the emphatic—a middle-class, Victorian complacency—it is all too true; Philistine is, in fact, the only word to fit the case; and yet, by dint of sheer power of writing, the Philistine has reached Parnassus. It is a curious occurrence, and deserves a closer examination.

What are the qualities that make a historian? Obviously these three—a capacity for absorbing facts, a capacity for stating them, and a point of

view. The two latter are connected, but not neces-
sarily inseparable. The late Professor Samuel
Gardiner, for instance, could absorb facts, and
he could state them; but he had no point of view;
and the result is that his book on the most exciting
period of English history resembles nothing so
much as a very large heap of sawdust. But a point
of view, it must be remembered, by no means implies sympathy. One might almost say that it implies the reverse. At any rate it is curious to observe
how many instances there are of great historians
who have been at daggers drawn with their subjects. Gibbon, a highly civilised scoffer, spent
twenty years of his life writing about barbarism
and superstition. Michelet was a romantic and a
republican; but his work on mediaeval France
and the Revolution is far inferior to his magnificent delineation of the classic and despotic centuries. Macaulay's great-nephew, Professor Trevelyan, has, it is true, written a delightful account
of the Italian Risorgimento, of which he is an
enthusiastic devotee. But, even here, the rule
seems to apply; one cannot but feel that Professor
Trevelyan's epic would have been still more delightful if it had contained a little of the salt of

criticism—if, in fact, he had not swallowed Garibaldi whole.

As for Macaulay's point of view, every one knows it was the Whig one. In reality this is simplifying too much; but, however we may describe it, there can be no doubt that Macaulay's vision was singularly alien to the England of the latter years of the seventeenth century. Like Gibbon, like Michelet, like the later Carlyle, he did not— to put it succinctly—understand what he was talking about. Charles II, James II—that whole strange age in which religion, debauchery, intellect, faction, wit and brutality seethed and bubbled together in such an extraordinary *olla podrida*—escaped him. He could see parts of it; but he could not see into the depths; and so much the better: he had his point of view. The definiteness, the fixity, of his position is what is remarkable. He seems to have been created *en bloc*. His manner never changed; as soon as he could write at all—at the age of eight—he wrote in the style of his History. The three main factors in his mental growth—the Clapham sect, Cambridge, Holland House—were not so much influences as suitable environments for the development of a

predetermined personality. Whatever had happened to him, he would always have been a
middle-class intellectual with Whig views. It is
possible, however, that he may actually have
gained something from Holland House. The modern habit of gently laughing at Whigs and Whiggery is based on a misconception. A certain *a
priori* stuffiness which seems to hang about that
atmosphere is in reality a Victorian innovation.
The true pre-Reform Bill Whig was a tremendous
aristocrat—the heir to a great tradition of intellectual independence and spiritual pride. When
the Hollands' son travelled as a youth in Italy he
calmly noted in his diary that some one he had
met had a face "almost as stupid as the Duke of
Wellington's"; the young Fox was a chip of the
old block. Such surroundings must have been
good for Macaulay. It was not only that they
supported his self-confidence—he had enough of
that already—but that they brought him into touch
with the severity, the grandeur, and the amenity
of an old civilisation. Without them he might have
been provincial or academic; but he was not so; on
every page of his work one sees the manifest signs
of the culture and the traffic of the great world.

Thus Macaulay's Whiggism was a composite affair—it was partly eighteenth century and partly Victorian. But the completeness with which it dominated him gave him his certainty of attitude and his clarity of vision. It enabled him to stand up against the confusion and frenzy of the seventeenth century and say, very loudly and very distinctly, what he thought of it. So far so good. The misfortune is that what he thought was not of a finer quality. The point of view is distinct enough, but it is without distinction; and Macaulay in consequence remains an excellent but not a supreme historian. His Whiggism was in itself a very serious drawback—not because it was a cause of bias, but because it was a symptom of crudity. The bias was of the wrong kind; it was the outcome of party politics, and the sad truth is that, in the long run, party politics become a bore. They did not, indeed, succeed in making Macaulay a bore; that was impossible; but, though he is never dull, one constantly feels that he might have been much more interesting. Too often he misses the really exciting, the really fascinating, point. And how can one fail to miss a great deal if one persists in considering the world

from one side or other of the House of Commons?
, A certain crudity, a certain coarseness of fibre
—the marks of a party politician—are particularly obvious in those character sketches of great
persons which form so important a part of Macaulay's History. Within their limits they are admirably done; but their limits are too narrow.
They lack colour; they are steel engravings—un-
satisfactory compromises between a portrait in
oils and a realistic snapshot. One has only to compare them with Clarendon's splendid present-
ments to realise their inadequacy. With what a
gorgeous sinuosity, with what a grandiose delicacy, the older master elaborates, through his
enormous sentences, the lineaments of a soul!
Beside them the skimpy lines and cheap contrasts of Macaulay's black and white are all too
obvious.

But the Whig politician was not only crude; he
was also, to a strange degree, ingenuous and com-
placent. A preposterous optimism fills his pages.
The Revolution of 1688 having succeeded, all was
well; Utopia was bound to follow; and it actually
had followed—in the reign of Victoria. Thus he
contrasts with delight, almost with awe, the state

of Torbay at the time of William's landing and its condition in 1850. In 1688 "the huts of plough-men and fishermen were thinly scattered over what is now the site of crowded marts and of lux-urious pavilions." A description of the modern Torquay becomes irresistible. "The inhabitants are about ten thousand in number. The newly-built churches and chapels, the baths and libraries, the hotels and public gardens, the infirmary and the museum, the white streets, rising terrace above terrace, the gay villas peeping from the midst of shrubberies and flower beds, present a spec-tacle widely different from any that in the seven-teenth century England could show." They do indeed.

The style is the mirror of the mind, and Ma-caulay's style is that of a debater. The hard points are driven home like nails with unfailing dex-terity; it is useless to hope for subtlety or refine-ment; one cannot hammer with delicacy. The repetitions, the antitheses, resemble revolving cog-wheels; and indeed the total result produces an effect which suggests the operations of a machine more than anything else—a comparison which, no doubt, would have delighted Macaulay. The

descriptive passages are the most deplorable. In
a set-piece, such as the account of Westminster
Hall at the impeachment of Hastings, all the hor-
rors of a remorseless rhetoric are made manifest.
From the time of Cicero downwards, the great
disadvantage of oratory has been that it never lets
one off. One must hear everything, however well
one knows it, and however obvious it is. For such
writers a dose of Stendhal is to be recommended.
Macaulay, however, would not have benefited by
the prescription, for he was a hopeless case. The
tonic pages of the *Chartreuse de Parme* would have
had no effect on him whatever. When he wished
to state that Schomberg was buried in Westminster Abbey, he *had* to say that "the illustrious
warrior" was laid in "that venerable abbey, hal-
lowed by the dust of many generations of princes,
heroes and poets." There is no escaping it; and
the incidental drawback that Schomberg was not
buried at Westminster at all, but in Dublin, is,
in comparison with the platitude of the style, of
very small importance.

The curiously metallic quality in Macaulay's
writing—its hardness of outline, its slightly hollow
ring—is so characteristic that it is difficult not to

see in it the indication of some profound psychological state. The stout square man with the prodigious memory and the inexhaustible capacity for conversation, was apparently a normal human being, except in one direction: he never married, and there seems no reason to suppose that he was ever in love. An entertaining essay might perhaps be written on the sexlessness of historians; but it would be entertaining and nothing more: we do not know enough either about the historians or sex. Yet, in Macaulay's case, one cannot resist the conclusion that the absence from his make-up of intense physical emotion brought a barrenness upon his style. His sentences have no warmth and no curves; the embracing fluidity of love is lacking. And it is noticeable how far more effective he is in his treatment of those whom he dislikes than of those whom he admires. His Marlborough is a fine villain. His James II is a caricature, with a queer vitality of its own—the vitality of a marionette. But his William of Orange is a failure —a lifeless image of waxwork perfection. Macaulay's inability to make his hero live—his refusal to make any attempt to illuminate the mysteries of that most obscure and singular character—epitomises all that is weakest in his work.

Probably the futility of his aesthetic judgments was another effect of the same cause. Whenever he writes of pure poetry—in the essay on Byron, for instance—he is plainly at sea; his lack of sensibility becomes painfully obvious. A true child of his age, he had a profound distrust, amounting at times to an actual hatred, of art. That Queen Mary should have ruined her father, turned him out of his kingdom, and seized his throne for herself—all that was no blemish at all on her character: was she not acting upon strictly Whig principles? But one fault she did have. She was responsible for "a frivolous and inelegant fashion." She was the first person in England to form "a vast collection of hideous images, and of vases on which houses, trees, bridges and mandarins were depicted in outrageous defiance of all the laws of perspective." Queen Mary, in fact, liked china; and that could not be forgiven her.

The weaknesses are obvious, and the strength, suitably enough, is obvious too. History is primarily a narrative, and in power of narration no one has ever surpassed Macaulay. In that he is a genius. When it comes to telling a story, his faults disappear or change into virtues. Narrowness becomes clarity, and crudity turns into force. The rhetoric of the style, from being the ornament of platitude, becomes the servant of excitement. Every word is valuable: there is no hesitation, no confusion, and no waste. It is clear from his journal that Macaulay realised the dominating importance of this side of his work. He laboured at his purely narrative passages for weeks at a time, with the result that they are masterpieces. Nobody who has once read them can ever forget his account of the trial of the Bishops, the siege of Derry, and the battle of Killiecrankie. To write so is to write magnificently, and if one has to be a Philistine to bring off those particular effects one can only say, so much the better for the Philistine. But it is not only in certain passages that Macaulay triumphs. His whole History is conditioned by a supreme sense of the narrative form. It presses on, with masterly precipitation, from start to finish. Everything falls into place. Unsatisfying characters, superficial descriptions, jejune reflections, are seen to be no longer of importance in themselves—they are merely stages in the development of the narrative. They are part of the pattern—the enthralling, ever-shifting pattern of the perfect kaleidoscope. A work of art? Yes, there is no denying it: the Philistine was also an artist. And there he is—squat, square and perpetually talking—on Parnassus.

Carlyle

MY GRANDFATHER, Edward Strachey, an An-
glo-Indian of cultivation and intelligence,
once accompanied Carlyle on an excursion to
Paris in pre-railroad days. At their destination
the postilion asked my grandfather for a tip; but
the reply—it is Carlyle who tells the story—was
a curt refusal, followed by the words—"Vous
avez drivé devilish slow." The reckless insularity
of this remark illustrates well enough the extraordinary change which had come over the English
governing classes since the eighteenth century.
Fifty years earlier a cultivated Englishman would
have piqued himself upon answering the postilion
in the idiom and the accent of Paris. But the
Napoleonic wars, the industrial revolution, the
romantic revival, the Victorian spirit, had brought
about a relapse from the cosmopolitan suavity of
eighteenth-century culture; the centrifugal forces,
always latent in English life, had triumphed, and
men's minds had shot off into the grooves of eccen-

tricity and provincialism. It is curious to notice the flux and reflux of these tendencies in the history of our literature: the divine amenity of Chaucer followed by the no less divine idiosyncrasy of the Elizabethans; the exquisite vigour of the eighteenth century followed by the rampant vigour of the nineteenth; and today the return once more towards the Latin elements in our culture, the revulsion from the Germanic influences which obsessed our grandfathers, the preference for what is swift, what is well arranged and what is not too good.

Carlyle was not an English gentleman, he was a Scotch peasant; and his insularity may be measured accordingly—by a simple sum in proportion. In his youth, no doubt, he had German preoccupations; but on the whole he is, with Dickens, probably the most complete example of a home growth which the British Islands have to offer to the world. The result is certainly remarkable. There is much to be said for the isolated productions of special soils; they are full of strength and character; their freedom from outside forces releases in them a spring of energy which leads, often enough, to astonishing consequences. In Carlyle's case the release was terrific. His vitality

burst out into an enormous exuberance, filling
volume after volume with essays, histories, memoirs and philosophisings, pouring itself abroad
through an immense correspondence, and erupt-
ing for eighty years in a perpetual flood of red-hot
conversation. The achievements of such a spirit
take one's breath away; one gazes in awe at the
serried row of heavy books on the shelf; one reads
on and on until one's eyes are blinded by the
endless glare of that aurora borealis, and one's
ears deafened by the roar and rattle of that inexhaustible artillery. Then one recovers—very
quickly. That is the drawback. The northern
lights, after all, seem to give out no heat, and the
great guns were only loaded with powder. So, at
any rate, it appears to a perverse generation. It
was all very well in the days when English gentlemen could say with perfect sang-froid "Vous avez
drivé devilish slow" to French postilions. Then
the hurricane that was Carlyle came into contact
with what was exactly appropriate to it—gnarled
oaks—solitary conifers; and the effect was sublime;
leaves whirled, branches crashed, and fathers of
the forest were uprooted. But nowadays it hurls
itself upon a congregation of tremulous reeds; they

180

bend down low, to the very earth, as the gale passes; and then immediately they spring up again, and are seen to be precisely as they were before.

The truth is that it is almost as fatal to have too much genius as too little. What was really valuable in Carlyle was ruined by his colossal powers and his unending energy. It is easy to perceive that, amid all the rest of his qualities, he was an artist. He had a profound relish for words; he had a sense of style which developed, gradually and consistently, into interesting and original manifestations; he had an imaginative eye; he had a grim satiric humour. This was an admirable outfit for an historian and a memoir writer, and it is safe to prophesy that whatever is permanent in Carlyle's work will be found in that section of his writings. But, unfortunately, the excellence, though it is undoubtedly there, is a fitful and fragmentary one. There are vivid flashes and phrases—visions thrown up out of the darkness of the past by the bull's-eye lantern of a stylistic imagination—Coleridge at Highgate, Maupertuis in Berlin, the grotesque image of the "sea-green Incorruptible"; there are passages of accomplished caricature, and climaxes of elaborately characteristic writing; and then the artist's hand falters, his eye wanders, his mind is distracted and led away. One has only to compare Carlyle with Tacitus to realise what a disadvantage it is to possess unlimited powers. The Roman master, undisturbed by other considerations, was able to devote himself entirely to the creation of a work of art. He triumphed: supremely conscious both of his capacities and his intentions, he built up a great design, which in all its parts was intense and beautiful. The Carlylean qualities—the satiric vision, the individual style—were his; but how differently he used them! He composed a tragedy, while Carlyle spent himself in melodrama; he made his strange sentences the expression of a profound personality, while Carlyle's were the vehicle of violence and eccentricity.

The stern child of Ecclefechan held artists in low repute, and no doubt would have been disgusted to learn that it was in that guise that he would win the esteem of posterity. He had higher views: surely he would be remembered as a prophet. And no doubt he had many of the qualifications for that profession—a loud voice, a bold face, and a bad temper. But unfortunately there

was one essential characteristic that he lacked—
he was not dishonoured in his own country. Instead of being put into a pit and covered with
opprobrium, he made a comfortable income, was
supplied by Mrs. Carlyle with everything that he
wanted, and was the favourite guest at Lady Ash-
burton's fashionable parties. Prophecies, in such
circumstances, however voluminous and disagree-
able they may be, are apt to have something
wrong with them. And, in any case, who remembers prophets? Isaiah and Jeremiah, no doubt,
have gained a certain reputation; but then Isaiah
and Jeremiah have had the extraordinary good
fortune to be translated into English by a com-
mittee of Elizabethan bishops.

To be a prophet is to be a moralist, and it was
the moral preoccupation in Carlyle's mind that
was particularly injurious to his artistic instincts.
In Latin countries—the fact is significant—morals
and manners are expressed by the same word; in
England it is not so; to some Britons, indeed, the
two notions appear to be positively antithetical.
Perhaps this is a mistake. Perhaps if Carlyle's
manners had been more polished his morals would
have been less distressing. Morality, curiously

enough, seems to belong to that class of things which are of the highest value, which perform a necessary function, which are, in fact, an essential part of the human mechanism, but which should only be referred to with the greatest circumspection. Carlyle had no notion that this was the case, and the result was disastrous. In his history, especially, it is impossible to escape from the devastating effects of his reckless moral sense.

Perhaps it is the platitude of such a state of mind that is its most exasperating quality. Surely, one thinks, poor Louis XV might be allowed to die without a sermon from Chelsea. But no! The opportunity must not be missed; the preacher draws a long breath, and expatiates with elaborate emphasis upon all that is most obvious about mortality, crowns, and the futility of self-indulgence. But an occasional platitude can be put up with; what is really intolerable is the all-pervadingness of the obsession. There are some German cooks who have a passion for caraway seeds: whatever dish they are preparing, from whipped cream to legs of mutton, they cannot keep them out. Very soon one begins to recognise the fatal flavour; one lies in horrified wait for it; it instantly

184

appears; and at last the faintest suspicion of caraway almost produces nausea. The histories of Carlyle (and no less, it may be observed in passing, the novels of Thackeray) arouse those identical sensations—the immediate recognition of the first approaches of the well-known whiff—the inevitable saturation—the heart that sinks and sinks. And, just as one sometimes feels that the cook was a good cook, and that the dish would have been done to a turn if only the caraway canister could have been kept out of reach, so one perceives that Carlyle had a true gift for history which was undone by his moralisations. There is an imaginative greatness in his conception of Cromwell, for instance, a vigour and a passion in the presentment of it; but all is spoilt by an overmastering desire to turn the strange Protector into a moral hero after Carlyle's own heart, so that after all the lines are blurred, the composition is confused, and the picture unconvincing.

But the most curious consequence of this predilection is to be seen in his Frederick the Great. In his later days Carlyle evolved a kind of supermorality by which all the most unpleasant qualities of human nature—egotism, insensitiveness, love of power—became the object of his religious adoration—a monstrous and inverted ethic, combining every possible disadvantage of virtue and of vice. He then, for some mysterious reason, pitched upon Frederick of Prussia as the great exemplar of this system, and devoted fourteen years of ceaseless labour to the elucidation of his history. Never was a misconception more complete. Frederick was in reality a knave of genius, a sceptical, eighteenth-century gambler with a strong will and a turn for organisation; and this was the creature whom Carlyle converted into an Ideal Man, a God-like Hero, a chosen instrument of the Eternal Powers. What the Eternal Powers would have done if a stray bullet had gone through Frederick's skull in the battle of Molwitz, Carlyle does not stop to inquire. By an ironical chance there happened to be two attractive elements in Frederick's mental outfit; he had a genuine passion for French literature, and he possessed a certain scurrilous wit, which constantly expressed itself in extremely truculent fashion. Fate could not have selected two more unfortunate qualities with which to grace a hero of Carlyle's. Carlyle considered French literature trash; and the kind

186

of joke that Frederick particularly relished filled him with profound aversion. A copy of Frederick's collected works still exists, with Carlyle's pencilled annotations in the margin. Some of the King's poetical compositions are far from proper; and it is amusing to observe the historian's exclamations of agitated regret whenever the Ideal Man alludes, in some mocking epigram, to his own or his friends' favourite peccadilloes. One can imagine, if Frederick were to return to earth for a moment and look over one's shoulder, his grin of fiendish delight.

The cruel Hohenzollern would certainly have laughed; but to gentler beings the spectacle of so much effort gone so utterly awry seems rather a matter for lamentation. The comedy of Carlyle's case topples over into tragedy—a tragedy of waste and unhappiness. If only he could have enjoyed himself! But he never did. Is it possible, one wonders, to bring forth anything that is worth bringing forth, without some pleasure—whatever pains there may be as well—in the parturition? One remembers Gibbon, cleaving his way, with such a magisterial gaiety, through the Decline and Fall of the Roman Empire. He, too, no doubt, understood very little of his subject; but all was well with him and with his work. Why was it? The answer seems to be—he understood something that, for his purposes, was more important even than the Roman Empire—himself. He knew his own nature, his powers, his limitations, his desires; he was the master of an inward harmony. From Carlyle such knowledge was hidden. Blindness is always tragic; but the blindness that brings mighty strength to baffled violence, towering aspirations to empty visions, and sublime self-confidence to bewilderment, remorse and misery, is terrible and pitiable indeed.

Unfortunately it was not only upon Carlyle himself that the doom descended. A woman of rare charm and brilliant powers was involved in his evil destiny. Regardless both of the demands of her temperament and the qualities of her spirit, he used her without scruple to subserve his own purposes, and made her as wretched as himself. She was his wife, and that was the end of the matter. She might have become a consummate writer or the ruler and inspirer of some fortunate social group; but all that was out of the question; was she not Mrs. Carlyle? It was her business to suppress her own instincts, to devote her whole life to the arrangement of his domestic comforts, to listen for days at a time, as she lay racked with illness on the sofa, to his descriptions of the battles of Frederick the Great. The time came when she felt that she could bear it no longer, and that at all hazards she must free herself from those stifling bonds. It is impossible not to wish that she had indeed fled as she intended with the unknown man of her choice. The blow to Carlyle's egoism would have been so dramatic, and the upheaval in that well-conducted world so satisfactory to contemplate! But, at the last moment, she changed her mind. Curiously enough, when it came to the point, it turned out that Mrs. Carlyle agreed with her husband. Even that bold spirit succumbed to the influences that surrounded it; she, too, was a mid-Victorian at heart. The woman's tragedy may be traced in those inimitable letters, whose intoxicating merriment flashes like lighting about the central figure, as it moves in sinister desolation against the background of a most peculiar age: an age of barbarism and prudery, of nobility and cheapness, of satisfaction and desperation; an age in which everything was discovered and nothing

189

known; an age in which all the outlines were tremendous and all the details sordid; when gas-jets
struggled feebly through the circumambient fog,
when the hour of dinner might be at any moment
between two and six, when the doses of rhubarb
were periodic and gigantic, when pet dogs threw
themselves out of upper storey windows, when
cooks reeled drunk in areas, when one sat for
hours with one's feet in dirty straw dragged along
the streets by horses, when an antimacassar was
on every chair, and the baths were minute tin
circles, and the beds were full of bugs and disasters.

After it was all over and his wife was dead,
Carlyle realised what had happened. But all that
he could do was to take refuge from the truth in
the vain vehemence of sentimental self-reproaches.
He committed his confessions to Froude without
sufficient instructions; and when he died he left
behind him a legacy of doubt and scandal. But
now, at length, some enjoyment appeared upon
the scene. No one was happier than Froude, with
an agitated conscience and a sense of duty that
involved the divulgation of dreadful domesticities;
while the Victorian public feasted upon the unexpected banquet to its heart's content.

Froude

JAMES ANTHONY FROUDE was one of the salient figures of mid-Victorian England. In that society of prepotent personages he more than held his own. He was not merely the author of the famous *History;* he was a man of letters who was also a man of the world, an accomplished gentleman, whose rich nature overflowed with abounding energy, a sportsman, a yachtsman, a brilliant and magnificent talker—and something more: one in whose presence it was impossible not to feel a hint of mystery, of strange melancholy, an uncomfortable suggestion of enigmatic power. His most impressive appearance completed the effect: the height, the long, pale face, the massive, vigorous features, the black hair and eyebrows, and the immense eyes, with their glowing darkness, whose colour—so a careful observer noted—was neither brown, nor blue, nor black, but red. What was the explanation of it all? What was the inner cause of this *brio* and this sadness, this passionate earnestness and this sardonic wit? One wonders, as his after-dinner listeners used to wonder, in the 'sixties, with a little shiver, while the port went round, and the ladies waited in the drawing-room.

Perhaps it is easier for us than for them to make, at any rate, a guess; for we know more of the facts, and we have our modern psychology to give us confidence. Perhaps the real explanation was old Mr. Froude, who was a hunting parson of a severely conventional type, with a marked talent for water-colours. Mrs. Froude had died early, leaving the boy to be brought up by this ironbound clergyman and some brothers much older than himself. His childhood was wretched, his boyhood was frightful. He was sent, ill and overgrown, to college at Westminster, and there—it was, as the biographers dutifully point out, in the bad old days before the influence of Dr. Arnold had turned the Public Schools into models of industry and civilised behaviour—he suffered, for two years, indescribable torment. He was removed in disgrace, flogged by his father for imaginary delinquencies, and kept at home for two years more in the condition of an outcast. His

eldest brother, Hurrell, who was one of the lead-
ers in the new fashion of taking Christianity seriously, and mortified his own flesh by eating fish
on Fridays, egged on the parental discipline with
pious glee. At last, grown too old for castigation,
the lad was allowed to go to Oxford. There, for
the first time in his life, he began to enjoy himself, and became engaged to an attractive young
lady. But he had run up bills with the Oxford
tradesmen, had told his father they were less than
they were, the facts had come out, and old Mr.
Froude, declaring that his son was little better
than a common swindler, denounced him as such
to the young lady's father, who thereupon broke
off the engagement. It seems surprising that Anthony resisted the temptation of suicide—that he
had the strength and the courage to outface his
misfortunes, to make a career for himself and become a highly successful man. What is more surprising is that his attitude towards his father never
ceased, from first to last, to be one of intense admiration. He might struggle, he might complain,
he might react, but he always, with a strange over-
powering instinctiveness, adored. Old Mr. Froude
had drawn a magic circle round his son, from

which escape was impossible; and the creature whose life had been almost ruined by his father's moral cruelty, who—to all appearances—had thrown off the yoke, and grown into maturity with the powerful, audacious, sceptical spirit of a free man, remained, in fact, in secret servitude—a disciplinarian, a Protestant, even a church-goer, to the very end.

Possibly the charm might have been exorcised by an invocation to science, but Froude remained curiously aloof from the dominating influence of his age; and instead, when his father had vanished, submitted himself to Carlyle. The substitution was symptomatic: the new father expressed in explicit dogma the unconscious teaching of the old. To the present generation Carlyle presents a curious problem—it is so very difficult to believe that real red-hot lava ever flowed from that dry neglected crater; but the present generation never heard Carlyle talk. For many years Froude heard little else: he became an evangelist; but when he produced his gospel it met, like some others, with a mixed reception. The Victorian public, unable to understand a form of hero-worship which laid bare the faults of the hero, was appalled, and refused to believe what was the simple fact—that Froude's adoration was of so complete a kind that it shrank with horror from the notion of omitting a single wart from the portrait. To us the warts are obvious: our only difficulty is to account for the adoration. However, since it led incidentally to the publication of Mrs. Carlyle's letters as well as her husband's, we can only be thankful.

The main work of Froude's life, the *History of England from the Fall of Wolsey to the Defeat of the Spanish Armada*, began to appear in 1856, and was completed in 1870. It is undoubtedly a deeply interesting book, full of thought, of imagination and of excitement, the product of great industry and great power of writing: whether it ranks among the small first class of histories is less certain. Contemporary critics found much to complain of in it, but their strictures were, on the whole, beside the mark. Among them the most formidable was Professor Freeman, who dissected Froude with the utmost savagery month after month and year after year in the pages of the *Saturday Review*. Freeman was a man of considerable learning, and of an ill temper even more considerable; his minute knowledge of the Early

English, his passionate devotion to the Anglo-Saxons, and his intimate conviction (supported by that of Dr. Stubbs), that he (with the possible exception of Dr. Stubbs) was the supreme historian, made a strange mixture in his mind, boiling and simmering together over the flames of a temperamental vexation. Unfortunately no particle of this heat ever reached his printed productions, which were remarkable for their soporific qualities and for containing no words but those of Anglo-Saxon descent. The spirit, not only of the school but of the Sunday school, was what animated those innumerable pages, adorning with a parochial earnestness the heavy burden of research. Naturally enough Froude's work, so coloured, so personal, so obviously written by somebody who was acquainted with the world as well as Oxford, acted like a red rag on the professor. He stormed, he stamped, his fiery and choleric beard shook with indignation. He declared that the book was a mass of inaccuracies and a dastardly attack upon the Church of England. The former accusation was the more important, and the professor devoted years to the proof of it. Unluckily for him, however, the years only revealed more and more clearly the indisputable value of Froude's work in the domain of pure erudition. He was not a careful transcriber, and he occasionally made a downright blunder; but such blemishes are of small moment compared with the immense addition he made to historical knowledge by his exploration and revelation of the manuscripts at Simancas. Froude was dignified; he kept silence for twenty years, and then replied to his tormentor in an article so crushing as to elicit something almost like an apology.

But he was more completely avenged in a very different and quite unexpected manner. Mr. Horace Round, a "burrower into wormholes" living in Brighton, suddenly emerged from the parchments among which he spent his life deliciously gnawing at the pedigrees of the proudest families of England, and in a series of articles fell upon Freeman with astonishing force. The attack was particularly serious because it was delivered at the strongest point in the professor's armour— his exactitude, his knowledge of his authorities, his undeviating attention to fact, and it was particularly galling because it was directed against the very crown and culmination of the professor's

history—his account of the Battle of Hastings.
With masterly skill Mr. Round showed that,
through a variety of errors, the whole nature of
the battle had been misunderstood and misrepre-
sented; more than that, he proved that the name
of "Senlac" with which Freeman had christened
it, and which he had imposed upon the learned
world, was utterly without foundation, and had
been arrived at by a foolish mistake. Mr. Round
was an obscure technician, but he deserves the
gratitude of Englishmen for having extirpated
that odious word from their vocabulary. The
effect of these articles on Freeman was alarming;
his blood boiled, but he positively made no reply.
For years the attacks continued, and for years
the professor was dumb. Fulminating rejoinders
rushed into his brain, only to be whisked away
again—they were not quite fulminating enough.
The most devastating article of all was written,
was set up in proof, but was not yet published; it
contained the *exposé* of "Senlac," and rumours of
its purport and approaching appearance were already flying about in museums and common-
rooms. Freeman was aghast at this last imperti-
nence; but still he nursed his wrath. Like King

Lear, he would do such things—what they were
yet he knew not—but they should be the terrors
of the earth. At last, silent and purple, he gathered his female attendants about him, and left
England for an infuriated holiday. There was an
ominous pause; and then the fell news reached
Brighton. The professor had gone pop in Spain.
Mr. Round, however, was remorseless, and published. It was left for his adversary's pupils and
admirers to struggle with him as best they could,
but they did so ineffectively; and he remained,
like the Normans, in possession of the field.

A true criticism of Froude's *History* implies a
wider view than Freeman's. The theme of the
book was the triumph of the Reformation in England—a theme not only intensely dramatic in itself, but one which raised a multitude of problems
of profound and perennial interest. Froude could
manage the drama (though in his hands it sometimes degenerated into melodrama) well enough:
it was his treatment of the philosophical issues that
was defective. Carlyle—it seems hardly credible—
actually believed that the Revolution was to be
explained as a punishment meted out to France
for her loose living in the eighteenth century; and

Froude's ethical conceptions, though they were not quite so crude, belonged to the same infantile species as his master's. The Protestants were right and the Catholics were wrong. Henry VIII enabled the Protestants to win, therefore Henry VIII was an admirable person: such was the kind of proposition by which Froude's attitude towards that period of vast and complicated import was determined. His Carlylean theories demanded a hero, and Henry VIII came pat to hand; he refused to see—what is plain to any impartial observer—that the Defender of the Faith combined in a peculiar manner the unpleasant vices of meanness and brutality; no! he made the Reformation—he saved England—he was a demi-god. How the execution of Catherine Howard—a young girl who amused herself—helped forward Protestant England, we are not told. Froude's insensitiveness to cruelty becomes, indeed, at times, almost pathological. When King and Parliament between them have a man boiled alive in Smithfield Market, he is favourably impressed; it is only when Protestants are tortured that there is talk of martyrdom. The bias, no doubt, gives a spice to the work, but it is a cheap spice—bought, one feels, at the Co-operative Stores. The Whiggery of Macaulay may be tiresome, but it has the flavour of an aristocracy about it, of a high intellectual tradition; while Froude's Protestantism is—there is really only one word for it—provincial.

A certain narrowness of thought and feeling: that may be forgiven, if it is expressed in a style of sufficient mastery. Froude was an able, a brilliant writer, copious and vivid, with a picturesque imagination and a fine command of narrative. His grand set-pieces—the execution of Somerset and Mary Queen of Scots, the end of Cranmer, the ruin of the Armada—go off magnificently, and cannot be forgotten; and, apart from these, the extraordinary succession of events assumes, as it flows through his pages, the thrilling lineaments of a great story, upon whose issue the most *blasé* reader is forced to hang entranced. Yet the supreme quality of style seems to be lacking. One is uneasily aware of a looseness in the texture, an absence of concentration in the presentment, a failure to fuse the *whole* material into organic life. Perhaps, after all, it is the intellect and the emotion that are at fault here too; perhaps when one is hoping for genius, it is only talent—only immense talent—that one finds. One thinks of the mysterious wisdom of Thucydides, of the terrific force of Tacitus, of the Gibbonian balance and lucidity and co-ordination—ah! to few, to very few, among historians is it granted to bring the κτῆμα ἐς ἀεί into the world. And yet . . . if only, one feels, this gifted, splendid man could have stepped back a little, could have withdrawn from the provinciality of Protestantism and the crudity of the Carlylean dogma, could have allowed himself, untrammelled, to play upon his subject with his native art and his native wit! Then, surely, he would have celebrated other virtues besides the unpleasant ones; he would have seen some drawbacks to power and patriotism, he would have preferred civilisation to fanaticism, and Queen Elizabeth to John Knox. He might even have written immortal English. But alas! these are vain speculations; old Mr. Froude would never have permitted anything of the sort.

Creighton

THE Church of England is one of the most extraordinary of institutions. An incredible concoction of Queen Elizabeth's, it still flourishes,
apparently, and for three hundred years has remained true to type. Or perhaps, in reality,
Queen Elizabeth had not very much to do with
it; perhaps she only gave, with her long, strong
fingers, the final twist to a stem that had been
growing for ages, deep-rooted in the national life.
Certainly our cathedrals—so careful and so un-
aesthetic, so class-conscious and so competent—
suggest that view of the case. English Gothic seems
to show that England was Anglican long before
the Reformation—as soon as she ceased to be
Norman, in fact. Pure piety, it cannot be denied,
has never been her Church's strong point. Angli-
canism has never produced—never could produce
—a St. Teresa. The characteristic great men of
the institution—Whitgift, Hooker, Laud, Butler,
Jowett—have always been remarkable for virtues

of a more secular kind: those of scholarship or of
administrative energy. Mandell Creighton was
(perhaps) the last of the long line. Perhaps; for
who can tell? It is difficult to believe that a man
of Creighton's attainments will ever again be
Bishop of London. That particular concatenation
seems to have required a set of causes to bring it
into existence—a state of society, a habit of mind
—which have become obsolete. But the whirligigs
of time are, indeed, unpredictable; and England,
some day or other, may well be blessed with
another Victorian Age.

In Creighton *both* the great qualities of Anglican
tradition were present to a remarkable degree.
It would be hard to say whether he were more
distinguished as a scholar or a man of affairs; but
—such is the rather unfair persistence of the written word—there can be little doubt that he will
be remembered chiefly as the historian of the
Papacy. Born when the world was becoming extremely scientific, he belonged to the post-Car-
lyle-and-Macaulay generation—the school of Oxford and Cambridge inquirers, who sought to
reconstruct the past solidly and patiently, with
nothing but facts to assist them—pure facts, un-

twisted by political or metaphysical bias and un-
coloured by romance. In this attempt Creighton
succeeded admirably. He was industrious, exact,
clear-headed, and possessed of a command over
words that was quite sufficient for his purposes.
He succeeded more completely than Professor
Samuel Gardiner, whose history of the Early
Stuarts and the Civil Wars was a contemporary
work. Gardiner did his best, but he was not an
absolute master of the method. Strive as he would,
he could not prevent himself, now and then, from
being a little sympathetic to one or other of his
personages; sometimes he positively alluded to a
physical circumstance; in short, humanity would
come creeping in. A mistake! For Professor Gardiner's feelings about mankind are not illuminating;
and the result is a slight blur. Creighton was made
of sterner stuff. In his work a perfectly grey light
prevails everywhere; there is not a single lapse
into psychological profundity; every trace of local
colour, every suggestion of personal passion, has
been studiously removed. In many ways all this
is a great comfort. One is not worried by moral
lectures or purple patches, and the field is kept
clear for what Creighton really excelled in—the

lucid exposition of complicated political transac-
tions, and the intricate movements of thought
with which they were accompanied. The biscuit
is certainly exceedingly dry; but at any rate there
are no weevils in it. As one reads, one gets to
relish, with a sober satisfaction, this plumless fare.
It begins to be very nearly a pleasure to follow
the intrigues of the great Councils, or to tread the
labyrinth of the theological theory of indulgences.
It is a curious cross-section of history that Creighton offers to the view. He has cut the great tree
so near to the ground that leaf and flower have
vanished; but he has worked his saw with such
steadiness and precision that every grain in the
wood is visible, and one can look *down* at the
mighty structure, revealed in all its complex so-
lidity like a map to the mind's eye.

Charming, indeed, are the ironies of history;
and not the least charming those that involve the
historian. It was very natural that Creighton, a
clever and studious clergyman of the Church of
England, should choose as the subject of his investigations that group of events which, centring
round the Italian popes, produced at last the
Reformation. The ironical fact was that those

events happened to take place in a world where
no clever and studious clergyman of the Church
of England had any business to be. "Sobriety,"
as he himself said, was his aim; but what could
sobriety do when faced with such figures as Savo-
narola, Caesar Borgia, Julius II, and Luther? It
could only look somewhere else. It is pleasant to
witness the high-minded husband and father, the
clever talker at Cambridge dinner tables, the industrious diocesan administrator, picking his way
with an air of calm detachment amid the reck-
lessness, the brutality, the fanaticism, the cynicism, the lasciviousness, of those Renaissance
spirits. "In his private life," Creighton says of
Alexander VI, "it is sufficiently clear that he was
at little pains to repress a strongly sensual nature. . . . We may hesitate to believe the worst
charges brought against him; but the evidence is
too strong to enable us to admit that even after
his accession to the papal office he discontinued
the irregularities of his previous life." There is
high comedy in such a tone on such a topic.
One can imagine the father of the Borgias, if
he could have read that sentence, throwing up
his hands in delighted amazement, and roar-

ing out the obscene blasphemy of his favourite oath.

The truth was that, in spite of his wits and his Oxford training, the admirable north-country middle-class stock, from which Creighton came, dominated his nature. His paradoxes might astound academical circles, his free speech might agitate the lesser clergy, but at heart he was absolutely sound. Even a friendship with that daemonic imp, Samuel Butler, left him uncorroded. He believed in the Real Presence. He was opposed to Home Rule. He read with grave attention the novels of Mrs. Humphry Ward. The emancipation of a Victorian bishop could never be as that of other men. The string that tied him to the peg of tradition might be quite a long one; but it was always there. Creighton enjoyed his little runs with the gusto and vitality that were invariably his. The sharp aquiline face, with the grizzled beard, the bald forehead, and the gold spectacles, gleamed and glistened, the long, slim form, so dapper in its episcopal gaiters, preened itself delightedly, as an epigram—a devastating epigram —shot off and exploded, and the Fulham teacups tinkled as they had never tinkled before. Then, a moment later, the guests gone, the firm mouth closed in severe determination; work was resumed. The duties of the day were dispatched swiftly; the vast and stormy diocese of London was controlled with extraordinary efficiency; while a punctual calmness reigned, for, however pressed and pestered, the Bishop was never known to fuss. Only once on a railway journey, when he believed that some valuable papers had gone astray, did his equanimity desert him. "Where's my black bag?" was his repeated inquiry. His mischievous children treasured up this single lapse; and, ever afterwards, "Where's my black bag?" was thrown across the table at the good-humoured prelate when his family was in a teasing mood.

When the fourth volume of the *History of the Papacy* appeared there was a curious little controversy, which illustrated Creighton's attitude to history and, indeed, to life. "It seems to me," he wrote in the preface, "neither necessary to moralise at every turn in historical writing, nor becoming to adopt an attitude of lofty superiority over any one who ever played a prominent part in European affairs, nor charitable to lavish undiscriminating censure on any man." The wrath of

Lord Acton was roused. He wrote a violent letter of protest. The learning of the eminent Catholic was at least equal to Creighton's, but he made no complaint upon matters of erudition; it was his moral sense that was outraged. Creighton, it seemed to him, had passed over, with inexcusable indifference, the persecution and intolerance of the mediaeval Church. The popes of the thirteenth and fourteenth centuries, he wrote, ". . . instituted a system of persecution. . . . It is the most conspicuous fact in the history of the mediaeval Papacy. . . . But what amazes and disables me is that you speak of the Papacy not as exercising a just severity, but as not exercising any severity. You ignore, you even deny, at least implicitly, the existence of the torture chamber and the stake. . . . Now the Liberals think persecution a crime of a worse order than adultery, and the acts done by Ximenes considerably worse than the entertainment of Roman courtesans by Alexander VI. The responsibility exists whether the thing permitted be good or bad. If the thing be criminal, then the authority permitting it bears the guilt. . . . You say that people in authority are not to be snubbed or sneered at from our pinnacle of conscious rectitude. I really don't know whether you exempt them because of their rank, or of their success and power, or of their date. . . . Historic responsibility has to make up for the want of legal responsibility. Power tends to corrupt, and absolute power corrupts absolutely. Great men are almost always bad." These words, surely, are magnificent. One sees with surprise and exhilaration the rôles reversed—the uncompromising fervour of Catholicism calling down fire from Heaven upon its own abominable popes and the worldly Protestantism that excused them. Creighton's reply was as Anglican as might have been expected. He hedged. One day, he wrote, John Bright had said, "If the people knew what sort of men statesmen were, they would rise and hang the whole lot of them." Next day Gladstone had said, "Statesmanship is the noblest way to serve mankind." "I am sufficient of a Hegelian to be able to combine both judgments; but the results of my combination cannot be expressed in the terms of the logic of Aristotle. . . . Society is an organism," etc. It is clear enough that his real difference with Lord Acton was not so much over the place of morals in history as over the nature of the historical acts upon which moral judgments are to be passed. The Bishop's imagination was not deeply stirred by the atrocities of the Inquisition; what interested him, what appealed to him, what he really understood, were the difficulties and the expedients of a man of affairs who found himself at the head of a great administration. He knew too well, with ritualists on one side and Kensitites on the other, the trials and troubles from which a clerical ruler had to extricate himself as best he could, not to sympathise (in his heart of hearts) with the clerical rulers of another age who had been clever enough to devise regulations for the elimination of heresy and schism, and strong enough to put those regulations into force.

He himself, however, was never a persecutor; his great practical intelligence prevented that. Firmly fixed in the English tradition of common sense, compromise and comprehension, he held on his way amid the shrieking of extremists with imperturbable moderation. One of his very last acts was to refuse to prosecute two recalcitrant clergymen who had persisted in burning incense in a forbidden manner. He knew that, in England

212

at any rate, persecution did not work. Elsewhere, perhaps, it might be different; in Russia, for instance. . . . There was an exciting moment in Creighton's life when he was sent to Moscow to represent the Church of England at the Coronation of the Emperor Nicholas; and his comments on that occasion were significant. Clad in a gorgeous cope of red and gold, with mitre and crozier, the English prelate attracted every eye. He thoroughly relished the fact; he tasted, too, to the full, the splendour of the great ceremonies and the extraordinary display of autocratic power. That there might have been some degree of spiritual squalor mixed with those magnificent appearances never seemed to occur to him. He was fascinated by the apparatus of a mighty organisation, and, with unerring instinct, made straight for the prime mover of it, the Chief Procurator of the Holy Synod, the sinister Pobiedonostzeff, with whom he struck up a warm friendship. He was presented to the Emperor and Empress, and found them charming. "I was treated with great distinction, as I was called in first. The Empress looked very nice, dressed in white silk." The aristocratic Acton would, no doubt, have viewed things in a different light. "Absolute power corrupts absolutely"—so he had said; but Creighton had forgotten the remark. He was no Daniel. He saw no Writing on the Wall.

The Bishop died in his prime, at the height of his success and energy, and was buried in St. Paul's Cathedral. Not far from his tomb, which a Victorian sculptor did his best to beautify, stands the strange effigy of John Donne, preaching, in his shroud, an incredible sermon upon mortality. Lingering in that corner, one's mind flashes oddly to other scenes and other persons. One passes down the mouldering street of Ferrara, and reaches an obscure church. In the half-light, from an inner door, an elderly humble nun approaches, indicating with her patois a marble slab in the pavement—a Latin inscription—the grave of Lucrezia Borgia. Mystery and oblivion were never united more pathetically. But there is another flash, and one is on a railway platform under the grey sky of England. A tall figure hurries by, spectacled and bearded, with swift clerical legs, and a voice—a competent, commanding, yet slightly agitated voice—says sharply: "Where's my black bag?"

214